Beyond Kegels

*Fabulous four exercises and more...
to prevent and treat incontinence.*

Janet A. Hulme, M.A., P.T.

Beyond Kegels, Fabulous four exercises and more... to prevent and treat incontinence.

Copyright © 1997 by Phoenix Publishing Co.

ISBN Number: 0-9644848-1-1

Design & Layout
Meerkat Graphics
Lolo, Montana

Published in the USA by
Phoenix Publishing Co.
P.O. Box 8231
Missoula, Montana 59807

ACKNOWLEDGEMENTS

Many thanks to Gail Nevin, P.T., Joyce Dougan P.T., Hilary Ort P.T., Gayle Cochran Pharm.D., Judy McDonald M.D., Jane Stansbury, and Linda West R.N., for assisting in the editing of this book; to my family, Erika, Abigail, and Richard for the time and encouragement to write, to the master editor for directing the final product, and to all my patients for providing essential information about what works and more importantly what does not.

TABLE OF CONTENTS

Chapter 1   Introduction 1
Chapter 2   How do I determine if leaking is
             a problem? 4
Chapter 3   Does anyone else have the same
             problem? *Case studies* 12
Chapter 4   What health care providers
             can help? 21
Chapter 5   How can I alter my personal
             and social environment? 28
Chapter 6   How is my body supposed to work? . . . 37
Chapter 7   What exercises can help?
             The Beyond Kegel Exercise
             Protocol for Incontinence 69
Chapter 8   What other techniques can help?
             Physiological quieting 96
Chapter 9   How does treatment for stress
             and urge incontinence differ? 100
Chapter 10   How can biofeedback help with
             exercise for incontinence? 102
Chapter 11   What are special considerations
             for special populations? 107
Chapter 12   What medications can help? 132
Chapter 13   How did exercise help?
             Case studies 139
Glossary of Terms 144
Organizations That Can Help 151
Videotapes/Audiotapes/Books 152

CHAPTER 1
INTRODUCTION

A newborn baby eliminates urine at will; the bladder empties without thought or inhibition. At the end of our life there is often the same pattern. But between the beginning and end of life, an important control function is toileting, releasing of urine at the appropriate time and place. Toileting is not talked about; often, excuses are made when someone has to go to the bathroom. Occasionally the comment is made, "I laughed so hard I wet my pants," or, "I was so scared I wet my pants."

Day-to-day, being dry and in control of when urine is released is expected in our society. It is assumed that everyone is dry as they perform their daily activities at home and in the community. If an individual experiences leaking, he/she often feels like "the only one," "the weak one," or "the inferior person." The truth is that twenty-five percent of adults 25-55 years old have experienced leaking problems at some time. One to two percent of adults leak at night. Thirty-five to forty percent of individuals over 65 who live in the community have leaking problems, and in nursing homes over fifty percent are incontinent. Even children have leaking problems: ten to fifteen percent of kids 8-16 years old have nighttime

1

wetting problems.

So the idea that between birth and death we do not have leaking problems is not true. The truth is, most of us at some time in our adult life, will experience some form of uncontrolled leaking (incontinence) that interferes with our daily activities.

Twenty-nine-year-old Mary leaks when she exercises, so she wears a pad and thinks there is nothing more she can do, because she had a baby two years ago and that's part of being a mother. Ruth is 59 years old and leaks when she tries to get in the door of her house after shopping. The urge to go is so great she cannot wait. "It's just part of menopause," she tells herself. Eighty-six-year-old Barron describes explosions of urine and some leaking when he is gardening or mowing his lawn. "It's part of getting so old and still being active," he tells his daughter as he refuses to see a doctor.

The idea that there is nothing to be done for leaking or incontinence is not true, either. A relatively simple evaluation by a health practitioner can indicate the appropriate level of treatment to eliminate the leaking in most cases. Medication, exercise, and biofeedback are the first treatments of choice. Surgery is needed for some more complicated conditions.

It is important that the individual experiencing the leaking begin to tell someone else about the problem. It may be another family member or friend at first. Just not keeping it a secret anymore is a big step. The next step is telling a health practitioner the details of the problem so an appropriate solution can be found.

2

In most cases exercise and self care routines are essential components of the solution to incontinence. In many cases exercise and self care routines, if adhered to on a regular basis, will eliminate leaking.

The primary purpose of this book is to describe and give rationale for the Beyond Kegel Exercise Protocol for preventing and eliminating incontinence. A secondary purpose of this book is to describe the self care routines that are important in solving the problem. Additional information on health professionals, evaluation procedures, medications, and adjunctive techniques that can help is provided.

The Beyond Kegel Exercise Protocol can be used as part of a general fitness exercise routine to prevent any incontinence problems. It is designed to significantly decrease or eliminate incontinence in those individuals who experience leaking caused by pelvic muscle dysfunction or bladder irritability. Exercises for incontinence are part of a total program of life-style change, physical fitness, education, and medication or surgery as indicated by special testing.

It is important to exercise under the guidance of a health care professional and to have an evaluation of the problem by a physician before starting any program.

CHAPTER 2
How Do I Determine If Leaking Is A Problem?

Any leaking of urine that results in life-style alterations, emotional changes, or feelings of discomfort is a problem.

Identifying the specific characteristics and severity of the leaking is the first step in finding a solution.

History Questions

An accurate history will help to define a specific type of incontinence which then allows for appropriate exercise, medication, behavioral, surgical intervention, and/or daily activity modification.

Describe the leaking problem in your own words by writing down the answers to the following questions:

How long have you had the leaking problem?

When does it occur?

How often do you leak urine in the daytime? In the nightime?

What makes it worse? What makes it better?

Have you changed your life because of the leaking?

4

The length of time that leaking has occurred indicates if it is an acute infection or other problem rather than a chronic, long-term problem.

When leaking occurs indicates external events that may precipitate leaking, and/or emotional factors that may be involved.

The severity of the problem is indicated by how frequently the leaking occurs. If the leaking occurs at night while lying down, it may be a more severe problem than if it is during the day when the individual is upright.

Identifying events that increase symptoms makes it possible to alter activities to prevent leaking. Noticing which events improve symptoms facilitates treatment planning to decrease incontinence.

Changes in daily activities indicate the impact of leaking on social and work contacts.

Characteristics of the leaking
Do you have trouble getting to the bathroom in time? In what situations?

Do you leak if you cough, sneeze, lift heavy objects, run, or jump?

Do you leak when you try to get in the door after shopping?

Do you leak when you get close to the bathroom?

Do you leak if you are in the shower or hear water running?

Do you leak when you have intercourse?

How large are the leaking episodes— a few drops or a large gush?

Types of incontinence

Stress incontinence is defined as leaking caused by increased intra-abdominal pressure, such as while coughing, sneezing, lifting heavy objects, running, or jumping. Leaks are usually in relatively small amounts.

Urge incontinence is defined as leaking in connection with a sudden feeling of need to toilet. There are relatively large amounts of urine lost. Individuals describe coming home and experiencing the sudden urge and leaking as the key is put in the door or when they get to the bathroom and see the toilet.

Mixed incontinence is a combination of urge and stress incontinence.

Overflow incontinence is defined as leaking from a full bladder because the bladder retains urine after toileting. It is usually caused by obstruction at the outlet of the bladder.

Functional incontinence is defined as the inability to void in an appropriate place due to physical disability or mental confusion.

Some women experience leaking primarily during intercourse. Since there is pressure on the bladder during intercourse, emptying the bladder prior to intercourse and then immediately afterwards is recommended.

Protection

What type(s) of protection do you use?

How many during the day? How many at night?

The number of pads used is one more indication of the severity of the problem.

Some individuals use toilet paper or paper towels alone or in addition to pads. How much is used indicates the severity of the problem.

Toileting

How frequently do you toilet during the day? How frequently at night?

What prompts you to go to the toilet?

When toileting, is there a strong or weak stream of urine?

Does your urine stop and start easily and completely?

How often do you have a bowel movement?

Do you have problems with constipation or diarrhea? How often?

The frequency of toileting indicates the irritability of the bladder and/or the autonomic nervous system that innervates the bladder.

The prompt for toileting can be a gentle or strong urge. It can be the individual telling himself/herself to toilet before leaving the home "just in case." Such frequent toileting decreases the size of the bladder, thus increasing the number of times the individual must toilet each day.

A weak stream of urine can indicate a urethral or bladder neck obstruction and/or pelvic and urogenital diaphragm muscle spasm.

Difficulty starting and stopping the flow of urine can indicate a neurological or muscular problem.

Any bowel problems can cause or exacerbate urinary problems. Constipation directly affects bladder irritability.

Daily fluid consumption

How much fluid do you consume a day? What kinds?

What is the pattern of your fluid consumption?

Have you changed your fluid consumption since the leaking started?

How much caffeine do you consume a day?

Six to eight glasses of liquid a day are recommended for bladder and body health. Too little or too much can cause problems. Too little concentrates the urine causing it to irritate the bladder. The bladder decreases in size due to decreased fluid intake. Too much liquid can cause leaking due to the great volume of fluid processing through the bladder.

Caffeine is a bladder and nervous system irritant. In some cases, eliminating caffeine can significantly decrease or even eliminate leaking.

Medical considerations

Have you had frequent bladder infections?

Do you experience pain or irritation with urination?

Is there blood in your urine?

What medication, over-the-counter and prescription,

are you taking? Do you consume alcohol?

What surgeries have you had? Give the date and results.

Have you had any medical intervention for incontinence before?

Frequent bladder infections are one precipitating factor in urinary incontinence.

Pain or irritation with urination can indicate infection, tumor, or muscle spasm.

Blood in the urine can indicate a foreign body, tumor, or infection in the urogenital system.

For Women

How many pregnancies, miscarriages, episiotomies, vaginal deliveries, and/or cesarean births have you had?

Were there any complications during the pregnancies?

Were you leaking urine during or after any pregnancy?

Have you been through or are you going through menopause?

Did menopause change your toileting pattern or urine leakage?

Pregnancy and childbirth cause stress to supportive ligaments and fascia. Damage can occur to the pudendal nerve during childbirth. It is common to have some transient incontinence during the last trimester of pregnancy and immediately after childbirth.

Menopause with its hormonal changes can cause incontinence, most often urge or mixed incontinence.

Now summarize the results of the history in a paragraph of six or seven sentences.

Daily Diary

The next step is to keep a diary for several days or a week. The diary will provide current information on toileting frequency, leaking episodes, fluid intake, and amount of protection used (Fig. 2-1).

The following diary can be copied and used. Under each day there are two-hour blocks of time. Record a "T" each time you urinate in the toilet, an "L" each time there is a small to medium leak, an "A" each time there is a large leak, a "G" each time there is an eight-ounce glass of fluid consumed and indicate if it is caffeinated by an asterisk (*), and a "P" if a new protective pad, etc., is used. Under comments, list activities and/or feelings that preceded leaks.

Summarize the diary results in a paragraph of five to seven sentences. How often are the leaking episodes? Do they occur during one part of the day more than another? Do they occur during one type of activity more than another? How many glasses of fluid are consumed in an average day? When is most of the fluid consumed? How much of it is caffeinated? How frequent are toileting episodes during the day, and at night? How many pads are used during the day, and at night? How wet is a pad when it is changed? Why is it changed?

Once the history and diary summary paragraphs are combined, a much clearer picture of the incontinence story is revealed. Based on this information, decisions about medical tests can be made.

The next chapter describes six individual's stories.

Weekly Bladder Diary

Name _____

Day_____ Date_____		Day_____ Date_____	
6-8am	_____	6-8am	_____
8-10	_____	8-10	_____
10-12	_____	10-12	_____
12-2pm	_____	12-2pm	_____
2-4	_____	2-4	_____
4-6	_____	4-6	_____
6-8	_____	6-8	_____
8-10	_____	8-10	_____
10-12	_____	10-12	_____
overnight	_____	overnight	_____
*pads used	_____	*pads used	_____
comments	_____	comments	_____
	_____		_____
	_____		_____
	_____		_____
	_____		_____

T=toilet   G=8oz. fluid   **Figure 2-1**

L=small leak   *=caffeinated

A=large leak   P=pad

CHAPTER 3

DOES ANYONE ELSE HAVE THE SAME PROBLEM?

Case Studies

Six individuals agreed to share their stories about incontinence. They tell about the characteristics of their incontinence, when it started, and what impact it had on their lives.

Each individual case has a unique history and pattern of incontinence, but there are also commonalities between the case studies. The case studies are presented with the intent that the reader may find similarities to his/her own story and be encouraged to read further for solutions to the leaking problem. After reading each case study, ask, "What similarities are there in this history and my problems?" "What differences are there?" After reading each succeeding chapter of this book, return to the case studies and ask, "How could this information apply to the problem described here?"

Each of the individuals in the case studies, under guidance of a health care professional, used exercise and self care routines to significantly decrease or eliminate the leaking problem. In chapter 13, the interventions used and the results obtained at the completion of treatment are described. So, after completing the book, you can compare your recommendations with the treatment protocols that were actually used and see the results of that treatment.

Lizzie, 9 years old: Bedwetting

Lizzie is a 9-year-old girl who experiences nighttime wetting (enuresis). She has been dry at night two times in her lifetime that she can remember. She attends a private school and is an accomplished student. She is also active in soccer and swimming.

Lizzie describes no problem getting to sleep or staying asleep at night. In fact, it is difficult for her to wake up enough to change the bed sheets and pajamas when she wets at night. Her mother puts clean sheets and pajamas beside her bed to use if she needs them. She describes feeling rested when she awakens in the morning.

During the day, Lizzie is dry. She toilets approximately every 2-4 hours. She has had no pain with urination and no bladder infections. There are no problems with constipation or diarrhea. She was toilet-trained for both bowel and bladder at approximately 2 years of age. Until she was about 6 years old, she had occasional problems getting to the bathroom in time during the day.

She describes worrying about wetting when she goes on swim team trips or for a sleepover with friends. She describes worrying about any odor she might have that would give her problem away at school. Her mother is concerned that Lizzie is becoming more isolated from her friends and sports teams because of the enuresis.

There is a history on both sides of the family of bed-wetting until puberty.

Mary, 29 years old: Stress Incontinence

Mary is 29 years old and began experiencing urinary leaking 15 months after the birth of her first child. The childbirth was complicated by a vaginal tear which was repaired surgically. Since that time, she leaks urine when she sneezes, coughs, or does any type of aerobic exercise in the standing position, i.e., brisk walking, running, dancing. She uses 3 pads a day. She toilets approximately every 2 hours during the day, and is up once or twice a night to toilet. Immediately after the childbirth and vaginal surgery, she had several bladder infections, but in the last 9 months she has been symptom-free.

At the present time, Mary works 6 hours a day as an accountant in addition to taking care of her daughter. She worked full-time before the childbirth and vaginal surgery. She tries to exercise at least 3 times a week for 30-45 minutes. She used to run 3-5 miles a day, but presently walks or exercises on a stationary bike.

She describes periodic back pain extending into her buttocks but not down her legs. Exercise seems to help the pain if she does it at the present level of 30-45 minutes, 3-4 days a week.

She describes being worried because the leaking is not decreasing with time. It limits her exercise, both the type of exercise she does and the length of time she can do it. She also is concerned that she will have to wear pads the rest of her life, and her image as a wife and lover is severely altered since the leaking started. Her husband has been understanding, but she feels as if she has to hide things about herself she did not before.

Erin, 32 years old: Stress Incontinence

Erin is 32 years old with a 3-year-old son and a job as an aerobics instructor at a health club. Erin teaches aerobics 3-4 times a week for 50 minutes. She works out daily, weight-lifting, running 3 miles a day, biking, or swimming. She golfs with her husband once a week and is in a golf league in the summer months.

Erin describes the leaking as having started about two years ago. It occurs as small leaks during aerobics and running. She wears a light pad during exercise. She leaks approximately three days a week.

Erin toilets every 3-4 hours. She drinks 2-3 colas a day and 2 cups of coffee in the morning. She drinks 5-6 glasses of water a day, usually while exercising. She consumes no alcohol and takes no medications.

Erin has had one live birth with no complications. She has regular menstrual cycles. Her body fat is 13 percent.

Erin is worried the problem leaking will increase as she gets older and if she has more children. She is planning to have at least one more child and wants to stay physically active the rest of her life.

Beth, 59 years old: Urge Incontinence

Beth is 59 years old and started leaking 3-4 years

ago. It began one day when, after shopping, she could not get the house door open fast enough to get to the bathroom before leaking. She would have a sudden urge to go and could not hold it until she reached the toilet. Initially it occurred once every 2-3 weeks. Now she experiences 4-5 urge incidents a day and leaking at least 2-3 times a day. Sometimes the loss of urine is significant. She has started wearing dark pants so the wetness won't show, because if she is out shopping and the bathroom is not close by, the pad she wears may not always be adequate to contain the leaking.

She gets up 2-3 times a night, usually awakening with the feeling that she needs to go to the toilet. She has leaked small amounts during the night on occasion. She uses 1-2 super absorbant pads during the day, and puts a towel under her at night.

She has had no bladder infections, has not experienced any pain during toileting, and has no back pain.

She drinks 6-8 cups of caffeinated coffee a day, most of it before noon. She limits her fluid intake after noon, drinking only 1 glass of milk at dinner. She states that she needs the coffee to get going in the morning, but she limits fluid in the afternoon and evening so she won't leak.

She had a hysterectomy at age 41 without complications and experienced no leaking at that time. She had 3 vaginal deliveries with no significant complications, between 20 and 30 years of age.

She has tried medication which helped some but did not cure the problem and it made her feel "spacey" and disoriented so she quit using it. She has done Kegel exercises for the last three years but they haven't seemed to help.

Beth is worried that the leaking is increasing as she ages. She describes it limiting her social life. She goes only to the grocery stores and department stores where she knows the bathroom locations. She used to like to travel but now has made excuses not to go on a vacation with friends because she worries about her leaking and all the pads she would have to take. She likes to garden but, because the garden is far away from the house, she has frequent leaking problems when gardening. She states humorously that she feels as if the next step may be the nursing home.

Matilda, 82 years old: Stress Incontinence

Matilda is a retired school teacher who describes leaking when she bends over, gets up from sitting, walks any distance, or places her hands under running water. She leaks at night when she gets up to go to the bathroom which is once or twice a night. She states the symptoms have been getting worse for the past 5 years but that she has had some leaking for at least 10 years. Matilda thought it was part of natural aging so she did not tell her doctor on her yearly visits about the problem until last year.

She lives alone in a condominium senior residence where she can cook for herself or go to a central dining room. She likes to exercise daily, walking the half-mile loop around the park on nice days, or riding the stationary bike in the exercise room of the social center. Matilda finds that the leaking is interfering with her exercise. She plays pinochle 2-3 times a week with friends at the social center or at one of their homes. She volunteers at the central dining room, taking meal tickets once a week. Her daughter's family takes her to church on Sunday and then out to dinner.

Matilda uses 2-3 super absorbant pads at night. She toilets every hour to try to keep from leaking. She drinks 3-4 cups of tea a day and a glass of orange juice in the morning. She does not like water.

Matilda finds that she has had to readjust her life in many ways to adapt to her leaking. She complains that she cannot go to church without getting up before the service is over to toilet. She has changed from wearing dresses to wearing sweat outfits in an attempt to get to the toilet more easily. She likes dresses and feels sloppy in sweat suits. She complains that she cannot exercise as much because of the leaking.

Robert, 75 years old: Radical Prostatectomy

Robert was diagnosed with prostate cancer 2 years ago and had radical prostatectomy surgery 18 months ago. He had chemotherapy after surgery.

His leaking has been constant since the surgery. He does not perceive the leaking itself but feels the pad getting wet. He describes the leaking as gushes and relatively constant. He leaks less at night but uses a pad. During the day, he uses 3-4 pads.

Robert says he was shown Kegel exercises by his

physician's nurse and has been exercising for the last year but has not noticed any difference in the leaking. He used to walk 2-3 miles day but no longer walks because of the leaking. Before the surgery, Robert helped at the senior center cleaning and setting up for meals. Now he leaks if he lifts tables or sweeps, so he has stopped going to the center because he feels helpless. Five years ago he married a woman 15 years his junior. They had planned to travel when she retired but now that is on hold.

Robert has trouble getting a good stream flow of urine when he tries to urinate in the toilet. He has no problems with constipation or diarrhea. His general health is good and all tests are normal. His leaking is keeping him home and isolated, a contrast to the extrovert his wife says she married.

Barron, 86 years old: Urge Incontinence

Barron describes being an active, healthy individual. He rarely goes to the doctor but did consult one for the first time in 8 years because of the leaking problems he is experiencing. In the last 2 years he describes experiencing a sudden urge to urinate and an inability to get to the toilet in time, even though he is very agile and active for his age. He does not leak during daily activities unless he has not gone to the bathroom for several hours and lifts heavy objects. Of more concern is the sudden "explosion" he can experience, where the urine leaks in relatively large amounts with very little warning.

Barron keeps active by caring for his own home, garden, and yard. He cooks his dinner but goes to the senior center for lunch. Barron is on the senior center board of directors and helps serve meals there as well. He walks a mile every morning after breakfast. His grandchildren live 3 hours away and he drives to see them frequently.

His physician prescribed a medication for the leaking but when Barron tried it he almost passed out, and his blood pressure, which was normal before, was significantly decreased.

Barron describes limiting how much he drinks and toileting every hour to try to control the frequency of the explosions. He experiences them once or twice a week. He uses a small washcloth in his underwear to absorb any leaking but says if there is a major explosion, it cannot hold it all.

CHAPTER 4

WHAT HEALTH CARE PROVIDERS CAN HELP? WHAT SPECIAL TESTS CAN BE DONE?

Many people with urinary incontinence do not tell anyone about the problem because they think there is nothing that can be done, or they are too embarrassed to say anything. It is important that the general public become more aware of the appropriate health care providers who can be of help to them. It is equally important that health care providers who routinely perform physical examinations and treat acute problems include urinary incontinence questions in the history portion of the evaluation.

Primary health care providers, such as family practice physicians, general practice physicians, internists, geriatricians, physicians' assistants, and nurse practitioners, can do the initial screening for incontinence in the form of several questions in the history portion of the evaluation or on a written questionnaire.

As recommended in Clinical Practice Guideline, No. 2, 1996 Update published by the Department of

Health and Human Services, physical examination, routinely done by a physician or other health care professional, includes the following:

1) Palpation of the abdomen for diastasis recti, masses, swelling or edema, tender or painful areas.

2) Genital examination in men to detect abnormalities of the foreskin, glans penis, and perineal skin condition.

3) Pelvic examination in women to evaluate perineal and genital skin condition, pelvic organ position, possible masses, pelvic muscle tone, etc.

4) General examination to detect possible neurological conditions such as multiple sclerosis, stroke, spinal cord compression, etc.; to assess independence of movement, mental status, and eye-hand coordination in the frail or functionally impaired; and to detect general edema or other systemic conditions.

5) Direct observation of urine loss. The individual is asked to cough strongly while the examiner observes urine loss. The test is done in supine but if no leakage is observed it is repeated in sitting and standing. If leakage happens with coughing, then stress incontinence is likely; if leaking is delayed or persists after coughing, urge incontinence is suspected.

Additional tests in an initial evaluation include the following:

1) Measurement of Post Void Residual Volume (PVR) using a pelvic ultrasound or catheterization. PVR is the urine left in the bladder after toileting. Before PVR is measured, the individual voids as completely as possible; the PVR is done within minutes

after the voiding. It is important that the individual be comfortable and relaxed during the voiding so the maximum urine is released before measuring the PVR. There is no documented normal PVR, but in general PVRs of less than 50 ml are considered adequate bladder emptying, and greater than 200 ml is considered inadequate.

2) Urinalysis is conducted to detect conditions, including infection, cancer, diabetes, or kidney stones. Careful cleaning of the genitalia with an antiseptic solution allows a "clean catch" of urine that can be analyzed.

According to the Clinical Practice Guideline, 1996, specialized tests are not part of the basic evaluation of urinary incontinence.

A specialist, usually a urologist, provides specialized tests that are not intended to be a part of the basic evaluation. These tests are appropriate after the basic evaluation and initial treatment in individuals who do not respond to that treatment or who are not appropriate for treatment based on the basic evaluation. Urologists are trained to perform specialized tests and surgical procedures of the urogenital system.

The specialized tests include urodynamic tests, endoscopic tests, and imaging tests.

Urodynamic Tests These tests are used to assess the anatomic and functional status of the bladder and urethra. When performing urodynamic testing, the urologist should attempt to reproduce the individual's symptoms.

Cystometry One part of urodynamic testing is

cystometry. This test measures bladder contractility with bladder filling. The bladder is filled to capacity using a urethral catheter, a plastic tube inserted in the urethra, and the action of the bladder muscle is measured.

Voiding Cystometrogram This is also called a pressure flow study. It can measure bladder contractility and pressure in the urethra as the individual urinates, which enables the evaluation of possible urethral obstruction.

Uroflowmetry This test measures the urine flow rate which may be helpful in individuals who have problems with bladder emptying. It is helpful in diagnosing some types of male incontinence.

Urethral Pressure Profilometry This measures resting pressure and dynamic pressure in the urethra. Sphincter function can also be assessed.

Electromyography This measures the nerve and muscle activity of sphincter muscles under the individual's voluntary control. Needle or surface electromyography can be used in association with a cystometrogram to aid in diagnosing specific types of incontinence.

Endoscopic Testing This test is performed when there is recent onset of irritable voiding symptoms, bladder pain, recurrent cystitis, a suspected foreign mass or blood in the urine without infection. The test performed is called a cystourethroscopy and is similar to an arthroscopy of the knee or shoulder joint. A miniature camera is placed in the bladder through the urethra. The urologist can assess the condition of the bladder, bladder wall, and bladder angle by observing the screen and taking video records of the test.

Imaging Tests X-ray and ultrasonographic imaging are the most common tests used for evaluation of anatomic conditions associated with urologic conditions.

Upper Tract Imaging Ultrasound of the kidneys, bladder, or both can help identify dilation of the upper urinary tract and kidney pathology.

Lower Tract Imaging This ultrasound of the urinary bladder and urethra, with and without voiding, is helpful in examining the anatomy of this area. This test can help in identifying bladder neck stability or mobility, urethral obstruction, and degree of cystocele.

Videourodynamics This technique combines the urodynamic tests with fluoroscopy and is used in complicated cases.

Physical therapists work with individuals experiencing incontinence in order to assess and treat any musculoskeletal component that may be a contributing factor. Dysfunction of the urogenital and pelvic diaphragm muscles often contribute to incontinence. Dysfunction of the breathing diaphragm, abdominal, and gluteal muscles can affect bladder control. A high percentage of individuals who are experiencing incontinence also suffer from back pain, hip pain or pelvic pain.

Accurate assessment and treatment of the back or hip pain can be an important part of treating incontinence because back and hip pain can be associated with nerves innervating the pelvic region. The presence of muscle dysfunction, such as rectus diastasis or piriformis spasm, is assessed and treated by the physical therapist simultaneously with re-education of the pelvic muscles to decrease or eliminate incontinence. Physical therapists, nurses, and psychologists with specialized training in biofeedback and incontinence evaluate and treat pelvic muscle dysfunction in connection with incontinence. Using evaluation skills ranging from observation to palpation to biofeedback, the therapist objectively quantifies the integrity of the pelvic muscles that support the internal organs of bladder, uterus, and bowel during rest and daily activities. Based on the evaluation results, the trained therapist outlines a progressive neuromuscular re-education and therapeutic exercise program designed to improve pelvic muscle function and to restore continence.

Observation of the pelvic muscle during bearing down or pushing indicates the presence and severity of a uterine prolapse, cystocele, rectocele, or enterocele. A uterine prolapse occurs when the uterus descends into the vaginal canal. A cystocele is a bulging of the bladder into a weak area of the vaginal wall. A rectocele is a bulging of the rectum into a weak vaginal wall. An enterocele is a protrusion of the pouch of Douglas into a weak vaginal wall. There are degrees of severity for each of these conditions. During pushing or bearing down, the uterus, bladder, or rectal bulge is observable through the vaginal opening in more severe cases.

Palpation of the pelvic muscles is performed to

assess strength and symmetry of the pelvic diaphragm and urogenital muscles. Two gloved fingers are inserted into the vagina or rectum to palpate muscle action. In the lithotomy position, the individual is instructed to:

1) Tighten the pelvic muscles quickly, then release them repeating six times;

2) Tighten the pelvic muscles and hold for ten seconds, then release/relax them for ten seconds. Repeat six times. Muscle strength can be graded on a 0-3 scale (Fig 4-1).

Pelvic Muscle Strength Rating Scale

	0	1	2	3
Pressure	None	Weak, feel pressure on sides of fingers, but not all around	Moderate, feel pressure all around	Strong, fingers compress/ override
Duration	None	< 1 second	1-3 seconds	> 3 seconds
Displacement in plane	None	Slight incline, base of fingers moves up	Greater incline, fingers move up along total length	Fingers move up and are drawn in

Figure 4-1

Biofeedback using surface, vaginal or rectal sensors assesses the pelvic muscles' function in supine, sitting, and standing positions. Resting level, quick contractions, and ten-second hold contractions are measured in microvolts of electrical activity coming from the nerve/muscle connection. Recruitment patterns and endurance of the pelvic muscles can also be assessed. Frequently, a second channel monitors the abdominal or gluteal muscles to assess accessory muscle use during attempted pelvic muscle contractions.

27

CHAPTER 5

How Can I Alter My Personal And Social Environment?

An individual with leaking problems changes his/her behavior to accommodate the leaking. Changes may occur in

1) what clothes are worn
2) what location and supplies are used for sleep
3) what activities outside the home are participated in
4) what food and drink are consumed
5) what friendships are maintained
6) what intimate relationships are maintained or entered into
7) what recreational or exercise activities are engaged in
8) what changes occur in self-concept and self-acceptance

Clothing

An individual experiencing incontinence will often wear only dark or black pants or skirts to hide any wetness. Clothing has to be cleaned often, so washable clothing must be purchased. Taking a change of clothes wherever one goes is easier if they are wash-and-wear

28

and lightweight so they can dry quickly and fit into a tote bag. Pants that are easily removed are important so leaking doesn't occur due to the delay caused by removing clothing.

Specialized, protective, reusable underpants are often worn in conjunction with incontinence pads. Other times, disposable briefs with absorbant pads are helpful. Some individuals use toweling, toilet paper, or sanitary pads to absorb leaks in regular underpants.

Nighttime

Some individuals have leaking problems at night. Various means of protection are used including an absorbant bed pad, towels placed on the bed, and specialized underpants and pads.

If leaking at night is prevalent, then some individuals report moving from sleeping with a partner to sleeping alone until the problem diminishes. Although difficult, it is important to communicate with a partner about feelings and facts as well as listening to his/her needs before this change is made.

At times individuals are getting up to toilet from several times a night to hourly. Sleep is severely disrupted and stress increases. Physiological quieting at bedtime and when the individual awakens in the night is helpful for this problem.

Food and drink

One of the most common comments heard when someone has a leaking problem is "I quit drinking much so I won't leak." Decreasing the liquid intake decreases the bladder size because the bladder stretches or shrinks depending on how much fluid is generally in it. As the bladder shrinks from less and less fluid being ingested, the brain is told it is "full" more frequently and the brain then tells the bladder to empty the urine more frequently. The result can be toileting routines that are every 30-60 minutes instead of the normal routine of every 2-4 hours. Less fluid also concentrates the urine with the result that the bladder wall is more likely to be irritated by the urine which often sets off bladder contractions. Instead of the common misconception that less fluid decreases leaking, the reality is that less fluid increases frequency of urination and bladder irritability, which often leads to more leaking. Therefore, drinking adequate fluid, six to eight, 8-ounce glasses, is recommended.

Alcoholic beverages are not recommended because they alter the nervous system controlling the bladder, and can be a bladder irritant. It is therefore important for individuals experiencing incontinence to eliminate alcoholic beverages from their diet.

Caffeine is a highly irritating substance to the nervous system controlling the bladder and bowel. The residue it leaves in urine is an irritant to the bladder wall. Eliminating caffeine, including coffee, sodas, teas, and chocolate, can decrease or eliminate incontinence.

Some individuals will use food as an emotional support or to cover up feelings when there is embarrassment and loss of control stemming from incontinence. The increased food intake leads to weight gain. Even a five-pound weight gain can have significant impact by increasing incontinence. The types of food we eat play as big a part in incontinence as the quantity we eat. Increasing the intake of fruits and vegetables will increase fluids and vitamin/mineral supplies while decreasing overall calorie intake. Eating unprocessed foods avoids chemicals that may be irritating to the bladder or nervous system.

Friendships

Isolation can be a problem when the individual with incontinence is embarrassed by the urine loss and is fearful someone will notice an offensive odor, a wet spot on his/her clothes, the bulge of pads used, or the frequency with which she/he uses the toilet. The ultimate fear is of a major accident when with friends or in public. It is important not to let these fears interfere with social activity. Outings with friends and family are essential to a happy, healthy life. Plan ahead, wear comfortable clothing, bring a change of clothing, wear pads or protective undergarments. Do whatever is necessary to be with friends and family.

It is important to tell friends about a leaking problem in a brief but informative way. "My bladder is malfunctioning so I need to use the bathroom frequently," is what Mona told her friend when they went shopping. Speaking up the first time is the hardest. It is important to maintain friendships since isolation leads to depression in even the healthiest person. Linda shared how she viewed her problem: "Incontinence is no different than poor eyesight. I use pads and do exercises for my leaking problem just like I wear glasses to improve my eyesight. Then I get on with my life, love, and happiness."

Intimate Relationships

Intimate relationships are an important consideration when dealing with incontinence. The partner in an established relationship needs to be informed about the problem and possible solutions in order to maintain physical and emotional closeness. Sharing feelings, both positive and negative, helps both partners continue the relationship. Try alternately listening to each other after asking the questions, "How do you feel about this leaking?" "What are the aspects you are comfortable with?" "What parts make you feel uncomfortable?" "What are your needs and how can I be involved?"

Expanding the definition of intimacy can be helpful in any relationship. Sometimes leaking occurs during intercourse. Using a plastic mattress pad or having intercourse in the hot tub or shower are options. Changing positions from the missionary position to sidelying or all fours with rear entry may put less pressure on the bladder.

Intimacy also includes physical hugging, caresses, and kissing; it can be verbal expressions of caring, it can be music, it can be movement in the form of dance, it can be fragrances in the environment, it can be the written word—25 reasons I love you, or a daily special note at the breakfast table. Intimacy can take many forms if we open our minds and hearts to love, and it should never be disrupted by a little leaking.

Recreational Activities

Maintaining an active and enjoyable lifestyle is an important aspect in treating incontinence. Physical exercise is vital to emotional and physical health. Physical exercise increases the endorphins—chemicals that elevate mood and are often called the "good humor hormones." Physical activity increases metabolism to help maintain weight control. Physical activity tones and strengthens muscles throughout the body. Too often, physical exercise is eliminated in an attempt not to leak. As 40-year-old Judy commented, "When I jogged or skied I leaked, so I quit jogging and skiing." Rather than quitting a favorite activity, it is important to make adaptations in order to continue the activity without embarrassment. Use a superabsorbant pad. Take breaks that allow time for toileting and plan ahead where the toilets will be. Bring extra clothing in case an accident occurs.

Incontinence can also be the impetus to try new activities. Instead of jogging Judy tried roller blading and bowling. She met new friends participating in these new acitivities and widened her perspective on what can be fun to do in her free time.

Self Concept and Self Esteem

Feelings of shame and embarrassment about leaking

often become generalized to the whole person, negatively affecting self-esteem. Common symptoms of depression include sadness, lack of energy, change in eating habits, and sleep disruption. Identifying with infantile or aging behavior rather than healthy, active adult behavior may be experienced. Confidence can turn to feelings of vulnerability, frustration, and anger. Examples of negative self-talk include, "I smell repulsive," "I can't go anywhere if the toilet isn't close by," "I act like a baby and treat myself like one," "If I were a stronger person, I could control this leaking," "My body is going downhill, losing control, and soon I'll be ready for a nursing home or the graveyard."

Active coping strategies are essential to positive self-esteem and self-concept.

1) Admit and identify the leaking problem.
2) Assertively gather information about your specific problem. Consult books, physicians, and support groups.
3) Consider all possible solutions before making educated decisions.
4) Develop and practice positive self-statements, such as, "I can make adaptations and go wherever I want," "I am an active, energetic adult who can solve a leaking problem," "I am a special person who deserves the best."
5) Practice self-reliance while changing life style habits that will facilitate being dry.

Getting Started and Keeping Track of Changes

To begin life style changes, pick two or three of the ideas just discussed and begin to implement them. For instance, the first week:

1) Eliminate all caffeine and alcohol, including colas, coffee, and chocolate.

2) Drink six to eight glasses of fluid a day to maintain the size of the bladder and also to dilute the concentration of urine.

3) Do some fun and purposeless activity every day. Twenty minutes of walking, swimming, or biking daily will help to strengthen the pelvic muscles and maintain overall good health.

To see progress, keep a daily journal. Record the glasses of fluid consumed, the caffeine consumed, the activity participated in, and the amount of time spent on the activity.

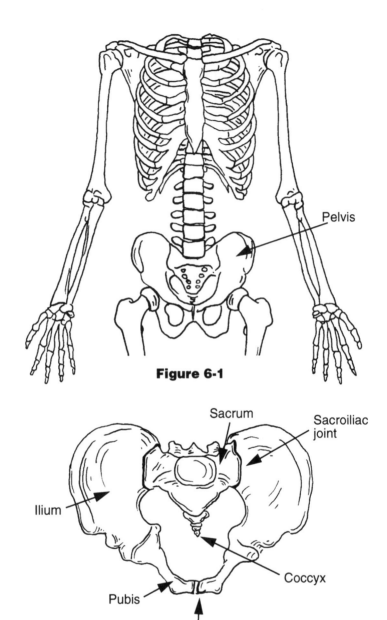

Figure 6-1

Figure 6-2

CHAPTER 6
How Is My Body Supposed To Work? Anatomy And Function Of The Urinary And Pelvic Muscles

The structures and functions of the urogenital and pelvic muscle systems are important to know when understanding the exercises to be done for urinary incontinence.

The Pelvis

The pelvis is the scaffolding for the organs and muscles involved in continence. The right and left sides of the pelvis are each divided into three parts: 1) the ilium, 2) the ischium, and 3) the pubis. The pelvis connects posteriorly with the sacrum at the sacroiliac joints. The pelvis connects anteriorly at the symphysis pubis joint.

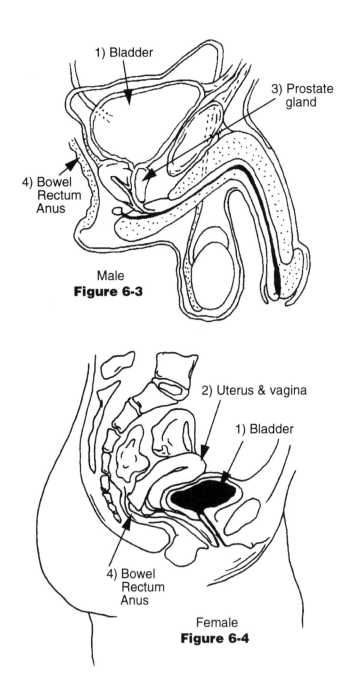

1) Bladder

3) Prostate gland

4) Bowel Rectum Anus

Male
Figure 6-3

2) Uterus & vagina

1) Bladder

4) Bowel Rectum Anus

Female
Figure 6-4

Pelvic Organs

The organs of the pelvis important in incontinence include:

1) bladder
2) uterus and vagina in women
3) prostate gland in men
4) bowel, rectum and anus

The bladder is located just behind the pubic symphysis. The uterus is positioned just behind the bladder. The bowel, rectum, and anus are positioned just behind the uterus.

The prostate gland in men surrounds the urethra close to the bladder neck. The bladder angle is the angle between the bladder and the urethra.

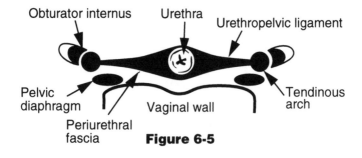

Obturator internus Urethra Urethropelvic ligament

Pelvic diaphragm Tendinous arch

Periurethral fascia Vaginal wall

Figure 6-5

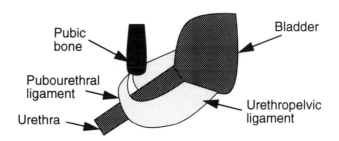

Pubic bone Bladder

Pubourethral ligament

Urethra Urethropelvic ligament

Figure 6-6

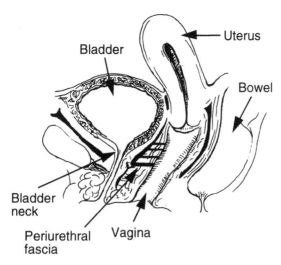

Bladder Uterus

Bowel

Bladder neck

Periurethral fascia Vagina

Figure 6-7

Fascial and Ligamentous Support

There is fascial and ligamentous support to maintain the bladder, uterus, and bowel in optimal position for function.

The urethropelvic ligaments stabilize and are the major support for the bladder neck and proximal urethra. These fibers originate on the obturator tendon (tendinous arch) in conjunction with the pelvic diaphragm/levator ani muscles and the obturator internus muscles. (Fig.6-5)

The pubourethral ligaments support and stabilize the mid-urethra. They attach to the pubic bone and surround the mid-urethral region. (Fig.6-6)

The periurethral fascia is a continuation of the ligamentous support and stabilization connecting the urethra and vagina. (Fig.6-7)

As the pelvic diaphram/levator ani and obturator internus muscles contract they elevate and increase tension on the tendinous arch which elevates the bladder via the urethropelvic ligament and periurethral fascia, which also attach to the tendinous arc and connect with fascia that encapsulate the levator ani muscles.

These fascial and ligamentous supportive structures help to maintain the bladder positioned up in the pelvis, the bladder neck stabilized, and the angle of the bladder and uterus forward toward the pubic bone. (Fig.6-7)

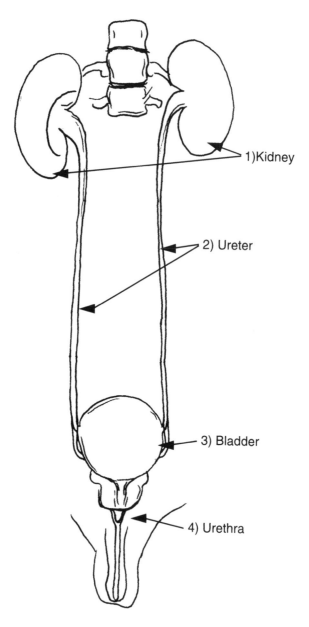

1) Kidney

2) Ureter

3) Bladder

4) Urethra

Figure 6-8

The Urinary System

The structures of the urinary system include
1) two kidneys
2) two ureters
3) bladder or detrusor muscle
4) urethra

The kidneys produce urine which is transported through the ureters to the bladder, a hollow muscular sack. The bladder expands to hold approximately one pint of fluid. It contracts to force the urine through the urethra to the outside.

The urethra, a hollow, muscle-lined tube is approximately the length of a thumb (5cm) in the female and the length of a straw (20cm) in males. The smooth muscle lining of the urethra contracts to keep urine in and relaxes to let urine flow out.

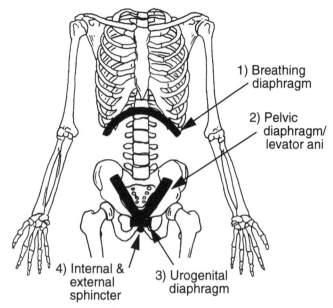

1) Breathing diaphragm

2) Pelvic diaphragm/ levator ani

3) Urogenital diaphragm

4) Internal & external sphincter

Figure 6-9

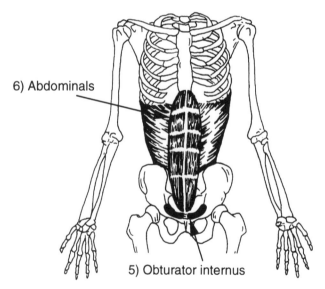

6) Abdominals

5) Obturator internus

Figure 6-10

The Skeletal Muscles

The skeletal muscles important in incontinence exercises include

1) breathing diaphragm
2) pelvic diaphragm/levator ani
3) urogenital diaphragm/perineum
4) internal and external sphincter
5) obturator internus (hip rotators)
6) abdominal (stomach)
7) adductors
8) gluteals

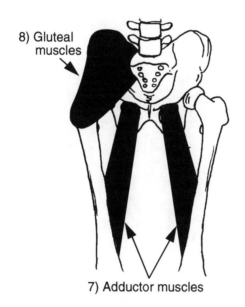

8) Gluteal muscles

7) Adductor muscles

Back View
Figure 6-11

45

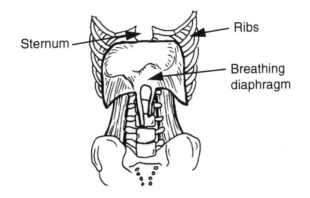

Figure 6-12

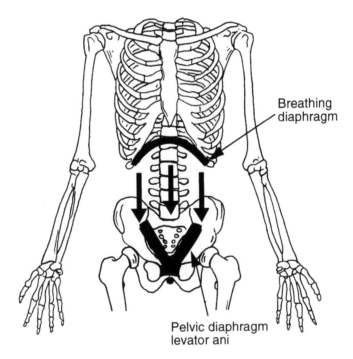

Sternum

Ribs

Breathing diaphragm

Breathing diaphragm

Pelvic diaphragm levator ani

Figure 6-13

The Breathing Diaphragm

The breathing diaphragm muscle sits below the ribs attaching to the sternum, ribs, and lumbar spine (Fig.6-12). During inhalation, the breathing diaphragm pulls down like a shade pulling down over a window; it compresses the abdominal contents and increases pressure on the bladder and bowel (increases intra-abdominal pressure) (Fig.6-13). During exhalation, the breathing diaphragm returns to the dome shape, decreasing the intra-abdominal pressure.

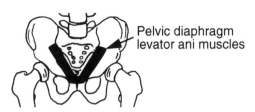

Figure 6-14

Pelvic diaphragm
levator ani muscles

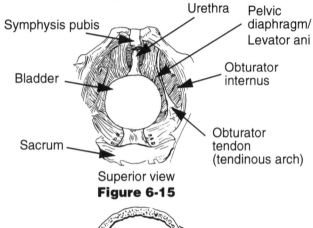

Symphysis pubis

Urethra

Pelvic
diaphragm/
Levator ani

Bladder

Obturator
internus

Sacrum

Obturator
tendon
(tendinous arch)

Superior view
Figure 6-15

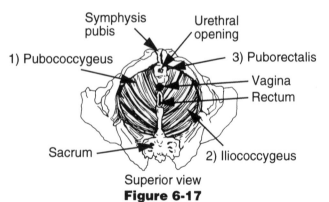

Bladder

Front View

Pelvic
diaphragm

Obturator
internus

Urogenital
diaphragm

Figure 6-16

Symphysis
pubis

Urethral
opening

1) Pubococcygeus

3) Puborectalis

Vagina
Rectum

Sacrum

2) Iliococcygeus

Superior view
Figure 6-17

48

The Pelvic Diaphragm/Levator Ani Muscles

The pelvic diaphragm, also known as the levator ani muscles, support and stabilize the internal organs of the bladder, uterus, and bowel (Fig. 6-14). The pelvic diaphragm muscles attach to the obturator tendon (tendinous arch), the pubis, the sacrum, and the inner surface of the pelvis (Fig. 6-15). During contraction of the pelvic diaphragm/levator ani muscles, there is increased support and stabilization of the bladder and bowel. There is improved closure of the urethral and anal sphincters (Fig.6-16).

The three muscles forming the pelvic diaphragm are the following:

1) pubococcygeal
2) iliococcygeal
3) ischiococcygeal or puborectalis (Fig.6-17)

The pubococcygeal muscle assists the urinary sphincter, the iliococcygeal assists in support of the vagina, and the ischiococcygeal or puborectalis assists the anal sphincter. They function in a sling-like fashion, maintaining a constant low level of contraction for postural support of internal organs.

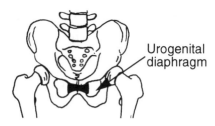

Urogenital diaphragm

Figure 6-18

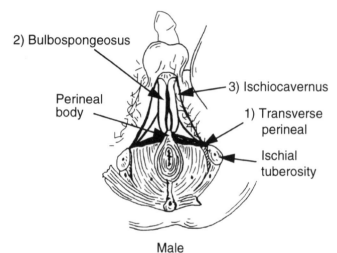

2) Bulbospongeosus

3) Ischiocavernus

Perineal body

1) Transverse perineal

Ischial tuberosity

Male
Figure 6-19

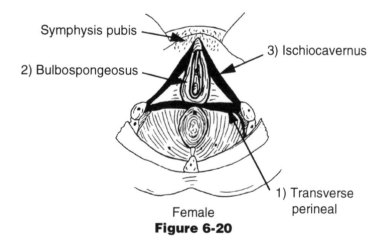

Symphysis pubis

3) Ischiocavernus

2) Bulbospongeosus

1) Transverse perineal

Female
Figure 6-20

The Urogenital Diaphragm/Perineum

The urogenital diaphragm, also called the perineum, is the more superficial diaphragm of muscles (Fig.6-18). It attaches to the symphysis pubis, pubic rami, the perineal body and the ischial tuberosities.

The urogenital diaphragm is composed of a triangle of three muscles (Fig.6-19 & 20):

1) transverse perineal
2) bulbospongeosus or bulbocavernus
3) ischiocavernus

They primarily assist with sexual function and urethral sphincter action.

Fast and Slow Twitch Fibers

Muscle fibers of the pelvic and urogenital diaphragms are divided into two types.

Fast twitch fibers, approximately 35%, act fast and intensely when coughing, sneezing, or doing something else unexpected that increases the pressure on the bladder and urethra. These fibers are like the leg muscles used during a sprint; they are powerful, explosive, and fatigue relatively quickly. The urogenital diaphragm and sphincter muscles are primarily fast twitch fibers used to stop sudden urine flow.

Slow twitch fibers, approximately 65%, act at a slow, constant rate of tightening for postural support. These fibers are like the calf muscles that maintain upright posture by contracting at a constant, low level. The pelvic diaphragm muscles are primarily slow twitch fibers supporting the bladder and urethra in optimum position for continence.

The pelvic and urogential diaphragm muscles act together somewhat like a hammock. In the resting position they gently support the internal organ structures. During physical activity or when there is a need to urinate and the toilet is not readily available, they tighten by pulling up and in much like a hammock pulls up and in when someone reclines in it. This hammock helps prevent leaking.

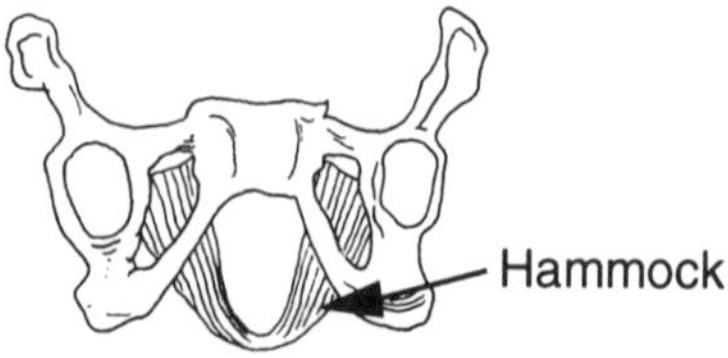

Figure 6-21

The Sphincter Muscles

The sphincter muscles include the following:
1) external urinary and anal sphincters
2) internal urinary and anal sphincters

The external sphincters are under voluntary control; an individual can open and close these circular muscles. They act like purse strings tightening to close off and stop urine or bowel movements until it is appropriate to release them.

The internal urinary sphincter in males and the bladder angle in females, and the internal anal sphincters in male and female, serve the same function but are not under our voluntary control. (In the female, the bladder angle functions as the internal urinary sphincter since an actual sphincter is not present.)

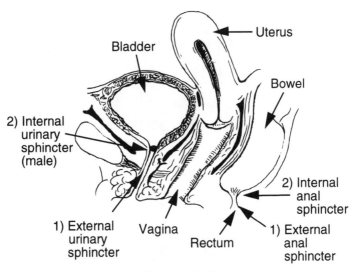

Figure 6-22

53

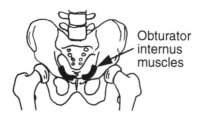

Obturator
internus
muscles

Figure 6-23

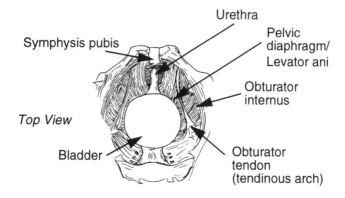

Urethra

Symphysis pubis

Pelvic
diaphragm/
Levator ani

Obturator
internus

Top View

Bladder

Obturator
tendon
(tendinous arch)

Figure 6-24

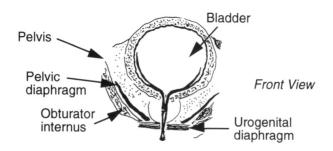

Bladder

Pelvis

Pelvic
diaphragm

Front View

Obturator
internus

Urogenital
diaphragm

Figure 6-25

Obturator Internus Muscle

The obturator internus muscle lines the internal surface of the lower pelvis and attaches to the obturator tendon (tendinous arch) within the pelvis and to the greater trochanter of the femur (leg bone) externally (Fig.6-23).

The obturator internus muscle attaches laterally and the levator ani attaches medially to the tendinous arch (Fig.6-24). The urethropelvic ligament and periurethral fascia which support the bladder and urethra surround the pelvic diaphragm/levator ani and also attach to the tendinous arch. So, as the oburator internus contracts, it acts as a pully lifting the bladder and urethra into position for optimum function through the tendinous arch, levator ani and fascial/ligamentous connections (Fig 6-25). The resting length of the obturator internus muscle also affects the bladder position in the pelvis.

Adductor Muscles

The adductor muscles attach to the pelvis close to the attachment of the urogenital and pelvic diaphragm muscles. The adductor muscles can facilitate action of the pelvic muscles as well as bringing the thighs toward each other.

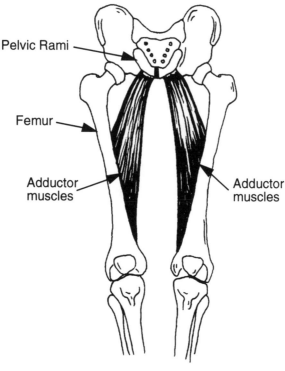

Pelvic Rami

Femur

Adductor muscles

Adductor muscles

Figure 6-26

Abdominal Muscles

The abdominal muscles are attached to the ribs, the sternum, and the pubic bone. They contract during lifting, pushing, and during rigid postural stance. During contraction, they increase intra-abdominal pressure, which increases pressure on the bladder, pelvic and urogenital diaphragm muscles.

If the abdominal muscles are chronically contracted, the breathing diaphragm cannot descend during inhalation. If the abdominal muscles are chronically contracted, there is constant pressure on the bladder, which can lead to bladder irritability and urge incontinence.

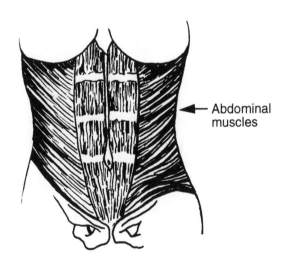

Abdominal muscles

Figure 6-27

57

Gluteal Muscles

The gluteal muscles attach to the posterior aspect of the pelvis and the sacrum as well as the femur (thigh). They are frequently tightened when attempting to contract the pelvic and urogenital diaphragm muscles to control leaking. Because they are a large muscle group, they can overpower the pelvic muscles, so the gluteal muscles should be relaxed during most exercises dealing with incontinence.

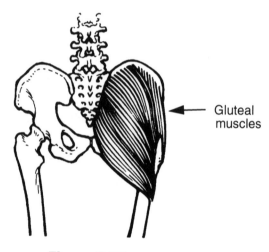

Gluteal muscles

Figure 6-28

Nervous System Involved in Bladder Control

There are two types of nervous systems involved in bladder control: the voluntary nervous system and the autonomic or automatic nervous system.

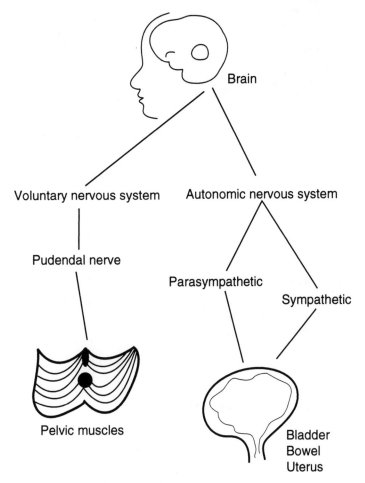

Figure 6-29

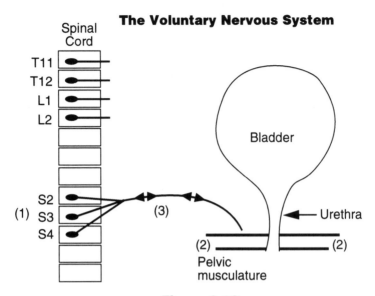

Figure 6-30

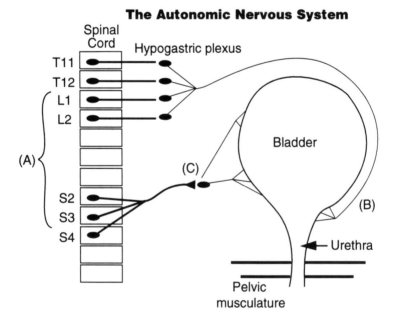

Figure 6-31

60

The Voluntary Nervous System

The voluntary nervous system, from sacral nerve roots two, three and four (1), sends and receives information from the pelvic and urogenital diaphragm and external sphincter muscles (2) via the pudendal nerve (3) (Fig. 6-30). This enables an individual to tighten and release these muscles on command. Because of this, it is possible, by lifting the muscles up and in, to strengthen them through exercise, because the nerves tell the muscles what to do through the voluntary nervous system.

The Autonomic Nervous System

The autonomic nervous system, coming from thoracic nerve roots 11, 12, and sacral nerve roots 2, 3, and 4 (A), is the automatic system not directly under an individual's control (Fig. 6-31). It sends and receives information from the bladder, urethra, bowel, and rectum.

The autonomic nervous system has two parts: the sympathetic system (fight or flight system), which controls the bladder neck and proximal urethra (B), and the parasympathetic system, which gives information to the brain about bladder fullness (C).

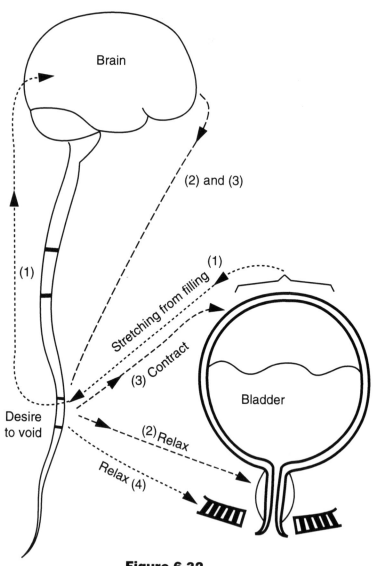

Figure 6-32

Bladder Emptying

As the bladder fills, it stretches, sending nerve messages to the brain telling how full the bladder is (1). The brain via the autonomic nervous system sends back messages to the bladder to release at the bladder neck and urethra (2) so the urine can flow out, and to contract gently at the bladder wall (3) to push the urine out. In men, there is more active bladder contraction to push urine out. In women, it is more a release of a tightened bladder neck and urethra.

During bladder emptying, the pelvic diaphragm, urogenital diaphragm, and external sphincter muscles relax at the direction of both the autonomic and the voluntary nervous systems (4).

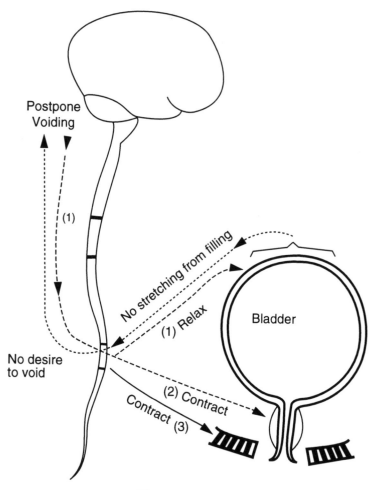

Figure 6-33

Bladder Filling

When the bladder is empty, the system quiets so the bladder can start filling again. The brain via the autonomic nervous system tells the bladder to relax (1). It tells the bladder angle and proximal urethra to tonically contract (2) so the urine can once more be stored in the bladder without leaking.

The pelvic diaphragm muscles, stimulated by the autonomic and voluntary nervous systems, return to a low level of tonic contraction which helps maintain continence (3).

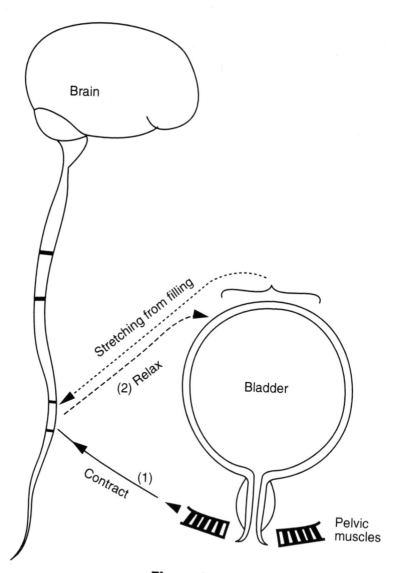

Brain

Stretching from filling

(2) Relax

Bladder

Contract (1)

Pelvic muscles

Figure 6-34

Reflex Connections

There is a reflex connection between the bladder muscle and the pelvic muscles. When an individual has the urge to urinate but needs to wait, the pelvic and urogenital diaphragm muscles contract to stop the urine flow (1). Nerve messages from the pelvic and urogenital diaphragm muscles to the bladder muscle tell the bladder to relax (2), thus keeping it from losing urine before the individual gets to a bathroom.

Much as when an individual moves his/her hand to the mouth (the biceps contracting and reflexively telling the triceps to relax so the elbow can move to bring the hand to the mouth), the pelvic muscles contract to keep the individual dry and reflexively tells the bladder muscle to relax until the toilet can be reached.

There are as many as sixteen reflex arcs between the bowel, bladder, spinal cord, and brain, all of which control continence of the bowel and bladder.

Stress and Urge Incontinence

If stress incontinence is a problem, (small to moderate amounts of urine are lost when an individual jumps, runs, coughs, or sneezes), the pelvic and urogenital diaphragm muscles' contraction is not fast or strong enough to overcome the urine pressure coming from the bladder.

If urge incontinence is a problem, (the sudden strong need to toilet before an individual can reach the bathroom), the bladder/detrusor muscle is contracting too frequently and at too great an intensity, thus over-coming the pelvic and urogenital diaphragm muscles so that a relatively large amount of urine is released before getting to the toilet.

CHAPTER 7

WHAT EXERCISES CAN HELP? THE BEYOND KEGEL EXERCISE PROTOCOL FOR TREATING INCONTINENCE

Since the late 1940s Kegel exercises have been recommended for treating incontinence. Initially the individual was instructed to tighten and release the pelvic muscles as often as 300-500 times a day. In the 1970s these exercises were encouraged in childbirth education classes when the instruction was to tighten and release the pelvic muscles 100-200 times a day. The instructor would say, "Every time you go to the refrigerator or are at a stop sign, do 10." By the late 1980s, Kegel exercises included quick contractions and ten-second-hold contractions practiced 20 minutes twice a day.

Originally little thought was given to other muscles contracting when the pelvic muscles tightened. The instruction was to tighten as much as possible. It was common for abdominal and gluteal muscles to tighten as much as the pelvic muscles. By the early 1990s the exercise prescription was to inhibit or prevent the abdominal and gluteal muscles tightening with pelvic muscle contraction. The instruction was to "keep your tummy and buttocks quiet and relaxed while you lift your pelvic muscles up and in." During this same period the concept of breath control with pelvic muscle contractions became important. Since breath-holding increases intra-abdominal pressure, bladder pressure, and leaking, the instructions were to "keep breathing while you tighten the pelvic muscles."

In the early 1990's, the typical exercise program included the following:

- quick contract and release of the pelvic muscles
- ten second hold, ten second rest of the pelvic muscles
- relaxed abdominal and buttocks muscles during pelvic muscle contraction
- breath control during pelvic muscle contractions
- 20 minute practice sessions twice a day

These exercises helped many individuals progress from constant or intermittent leaking to being dry in 6-12 weeks. They were primarily recommended for stress incontinence problems, relatively small leaks when coughing, running, jumping, lifting, or bending. Urge incontinence was not thought to be treatable through exercise.

In the last 3 to 5 years, new exercise protocols have evolved based on the historical information previously discussed and new perspectives on the anatomy and function of the urinary and pelvic muscle systems.

The Beyond Kegels Exercise Protocol is described in this chapter. The exercise protocol is designed to prevent and treat stress and urge incontinence. It was developed at Phoenix Physical Therapy's Continence Clinic with patients' input and analysis of patient data to determine which exercises and sequence produced the fastest and most lasting results.

The first four exercises have been named "The Fabulous Four" by patients because many patients are dry after completing these in the sequence outlined.

Before undertaking the exercises, there are several training principles important to remember in any incontinence exercise program.

Training Principles of Exercise
1) Overload Principle
2) Specificity Principle
3) Maintenance Principle
4) Reversibility Principle

The *overload principle* states that for pelvic muscles to strengthen, they must be pushed to the limit and just a little beyond. If over-exercised, the muscles fatigue and cannot function, so other muscles must try to compensate. The abdominal and gluteal muscles will become more active when the pelvic muscles fatigue. If the muscles are under-exercised, they are not challenged to increase in strength, endurance, or speed. Their length and resting tone remain the same.

The *specificity principle* states that the pelvic muscles

71

are composed of fast twitch and slow twitch fibers roughly in a 35%/65% ratio. Some fibers have a combination of fast and slow twitch components. Fast twitch fibers improve in speed and strength with quick explosive contractions, while slow twitch fibers strengthen and gain optimal resting length and tone with longer "hold" contractions, (10 second hold, 10 second rest periods rather than 1-2 second hold and rest periods). Fast twitch fibers fatique quickly, slow twitch fibers are designed for endurance and postural tone, so repetitions are low in number for fast twitch fibers and higher for slow twitch fibers.

The *maintenance principle* describes exercising for continence as a lifelong endeavor. Once a person is dry, the pelvic muscle strength is maintained by one session daily at a level of exercise that maintains continence, usually for 7 to 10 minutes a day. The pelvic muscles are no different than leg, heart, or lung muscles; they need exercise daily to remain in shape.

The *reversibility principle* states that if, after an individual exercises and becomes dry or continent, she/he then quits exercising, it will take three times as long for the pelvic muscles to return to their original strength as it did to reach the continent level of strength. For example, if it took three months to exercise to the point of continence, it will take nine months of not exercising to decrease tone and strength of the pelvic muscles to again experience leaking.

Exercising consistently and effectively is an important commitment. The Beyond Kegels Exercise Protocol is developed in eight levels for that purpose. The levels are designed to progress in body awareness, muscle fiber type, and level of exercise difficulty. It is recommended that an individual start with the Fabulous Four Exercises, the first four levels of exercise in the Beyond Kegel Exercise Protocol. Begin with Level One, even though it seems very simple, and progress sequentially until there is no leaking for 1 to 2 weeks.

Level One, Relaxed Awareness of the Pelvic Muscles, sets the stage for integrating body awareness and breathing with beginning pelvic muscle exercises. Levels Two and Four strengthen the slow twitch, postural fibers of the pelvic diaphragm/levator ani and obturator internus muscles. Level Three strengthens the fast twitch fibers primarily of the urogenital diaphragm muscles. Advanced Techniques are included in Levels Five through Eight. Level Five strengthens the pelvic muscle and obturator internus muscles in standing. Level Six, Seven, and Eight include advanced techniques involving breathing patterns, coughing, sneezing, and eccentric and concentric contractions.

Exercise Length and Duration are determined by the results of the initial evaluation of pelvic muscle strength. In general, start by exercising as follows:

First Week:	3-5 minutes, 3 times a day
Second Week:	5-7 minutes, 3 times a day
Third Week:	7-10 minutes, 2 times a day
Fourth Week:	10 minutes, 2 times a day

BEYOND KEGELS:
FABULOUS FOUR EXERCISES AND MORE...
TO PREVENT AND TREAT INCONTINENCE
Level One
Relaxed Awareness of the Pelvic Muscles

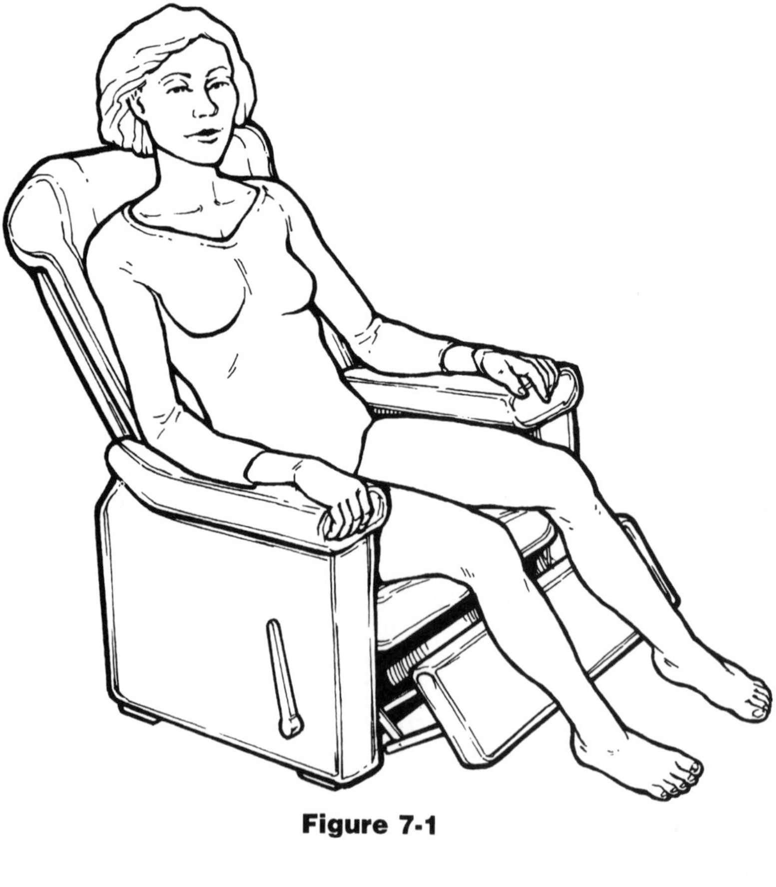

Figure 7-1

The first level is relaxed awareness of the pelvic muscles. In a comfortable, supported position reclining on a bed or semisitting or sitting in a chair, concentrate on the feel of the support of the chair or bed from your head to your feet. Feel that support and relax into that support, letting go into the support more and more through your head and neck, shoulders and back, arms and hands; let your hips and legs sink into the support, let your ankles and feet relax and release into the bed or the chair.

Now notice your breathing. Notice the natural rhythm of your breathing. Inhale.....Exhale...... Think, "Quiet shoulders, quiet chest." Let your stomach rise with your inhale, fall with your exhale. Now notice your stomach muscles and your buttocks muscles. Let them be relaxed and totally released as you do these steps. Connect your mind now to the hammock of muscle that forms the base of the pelvis, the hammock of muscle running from the symphysis pubis in the front to the tail bone or coccyx in the back. Maintaining your breathing rhythm, gently tighten this hammock of muscle, gently lift up and in to tighten, then release, gently and easily. Try again, tighten and release, maintaining your breathing, keeping your stomach and buttocks relaxed. Do 3 or 4 of these gentle contractions, keeping your mind connected to the hammock of muscle.

Practice this exercise for short periods 2-3 times a day, until it feels easy to tighten the pelvic muscles gently while keeping the buttocks and stomach muscles quiet and maintaining your normal breathing rhythm.

Level Two
Assisted Pelvic Muscle Tightening

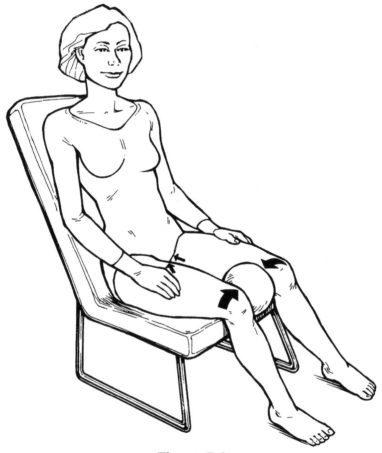

Figure 7-2

Using Adductors/Inner Thigh Muscles

For this exercise you will be using a toilet paper roll or a 7"-9" soft ball. Place the ball between your legs just above the knees. Now roll your knees in against the ball while lifting your pelvic muscles up and in, tightening around the anal and urethral opening, and tightening around the vaginal opening if you are a female. Hold for a count of 10. Now relax and release your knees, the pelvic muscles, your hips and buttocks, your back, neck, and head for a count of 10. Remember, as you do this exercise, to maintain your breathing rhythm, and tighten just the muscles of your inner thighs and the hammock of pelvic muscles. The muscles of your abdomen and buttocks should remain relaxed and loose.

Repeat this exercise 2-3 times a day for 3-5 minutes. If the muscles tire, do them for less time. Continue until this exercise is easy to do. This will often take 5-7 days. Then progress to the next exercise in this level.

Level Two
Assisted Pelvic Muscle Tightening

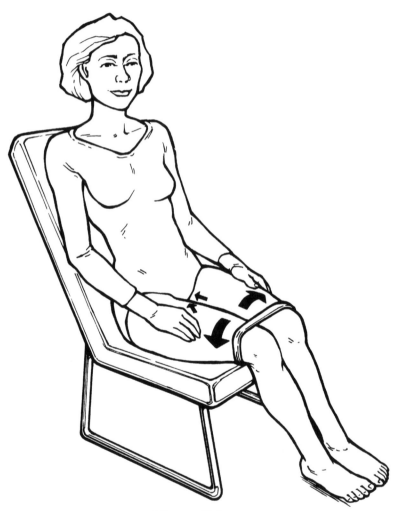

Figure 7-3

Using Obturator Internus Muscles/Hip Rotators

This level of exercise assists the pelvic diaphragm/ lavator ani muscles by using the obturator internus muscle. In this exercise, an elastic band 1"-2" wide is secured around the legs just above the knees. Now roll your knees out against the elastic band while you lift the pelvic muscles up and in, tightening the anal and urethral areas, and vaginal area if appropriate. Hold the position while you count to 10 slowly. Then relax the muscles completely, release your knees, and release your pelvic muscles for a count of 10. Maintaining your breathing rhythm, try this exercise again. Remember that rolling your knees out while using the small hip rotator muscles (the obturator internus), assists the pelvic diaphragm/levator ani muscles in support and stabilization of the bladder, urethra, and bowel.

Repeat this exercise 2-3 times a day for 3-5 minutes. When it is easy to do, progress to the next exercise in this level.

Level Two
Combining Inner and Outer Thigh Muscles

Adductor and obturator muscle assist-exercises will now be combined into one. Begin this exercise when the other two are easy to do. This exercise then becomes the only exercise done for Level Two.

Roll your knees in against the soft ball while pulling up and in with the pelvic muscles, holding for a count of 10. Then release and relax for a count of 10. Repeat this exercise 5 times.

Now roll your knees out against the elastic band while pulling up and in with the pelvic muscles, and hold for a count of 10. Then relax and release for a count of 10. Repeat this exercise 5 times.

Repeat the sequence 2-3 times a day for 5-7 minutes.

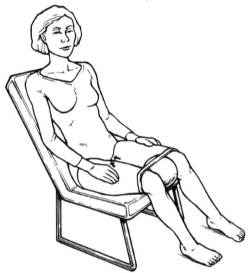

Figure 7-4

Level Three
Quick Contract and Release of the Pelvic Muscles

The exercise in this level improves the strength and function of the fast acting fibers primarily of the urogenital diaphragm and external sphincter muscles. These fibers are important for prevention of leaking during coughing, sneezing, lifting, and pulling, because these fibers act with speed and intensity to maintain urinary control.

To perform this exercise, focus on your breathing rhythm. Now maintain that breathing rhythm while you contract the pelvic muscles quickly and forcefully. Tighten at the rectal and urethral openings (and vaginal opening if appropriate) simultaneously, and then quickly release. Think or say, "Tighten.....and release."(Fig.7-5) It is as important to release completely and quickly as it is to tighten forcefully. It is also important that the pelvic muscles do the work while the gluteals, abdominals, adductors, and obturator internus muscles remain relaxed.

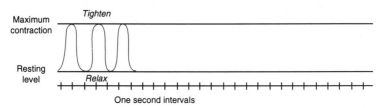

Figure 7-5

Perform 5-10 repetitions of this exercise at the beginning and end of each exercise session.

Level Four
Independent Pelvic Muscle Exercises

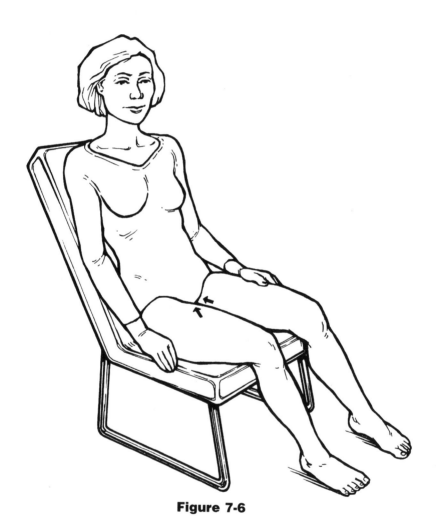

Figure 7-6

When Level Two Assisted Pelvic Muscle Exercises are easy, it is appropriate to exercise the pelvic muscles in isolation from the inner and outer thigh muscles.

Tighten(contract) the pelvic muscles, lifting up and in, without tightening any other muscles. Maintain slow, low breathing as you do this. Pull up and in with the pelvic muscles and hold for a count of 5 to begin with. Then relax for a count of 10. Notice that you hold this exercise for a count of 5 initially because the pelvic muscles get tired faster when contracting alone; they fatigue more easily at first. As they become stronger, you can hold for a count of 10 and relax for a count of 10.

Repeat this exercise 4-5 times. Gradually increase the repetitions to 10 as the pelvic muscles become stronger. First, increase the number of seconds you hold the contraction. When you can hold the contractions for 10 seconds, then begin to increase the number of repetitions.

Combine this level of exercise with the others, practicing 7-10 minutes 2 times a day.

ADVANCED EXERCISES

Level Five
Standing Exercises

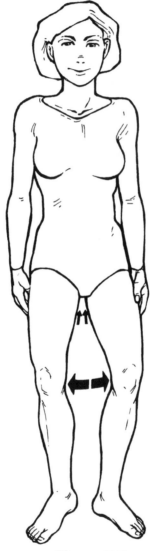

Figure 7-7

Combining Obturator Internus and Pelvic Muscles

Because much of our lives we spend standing, the pelvic diaphragm/levator ani and obturator internus muscles must have adequate strength and endurance in this position to prevent leaking.

Stand with your feet slightly more than hip-width apart with your feet turned outward. Now do a plié, bending the knees 2"-3" as you pull up and in with the pelvic muscles. Hold for a count of 10. Then return to the upright position and relax for a count of 10. The knee-bend position with the feet pointed outward brings in the action of the obturator internus muscle in combination with the pelvic diaphragm/levator ani muscles. Maintain slow, low breathing while doing this exercise.

Repeat this exercise 3-4 times initially. Gradually increase to 10 repetitions during an exercise session. This is a good exercise to do while standing in line at the grocery store or movies.

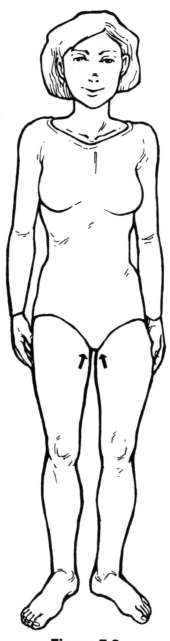

Figure 7-8

Isolated Pelvic Muscles in Standing

The next exercise in this progression is isolated pelvic muscle contraction while standing. Tighten the pelvic muscles in isolation from all other muscles while in the standing position. Pull up and in while breathing and count slowly to 5, then release and relax for a count of 10. Repeat 3-5 times initially.

Combine this level of exercise with the others, practicing 2-3 times a day for 7-10 minutes.

Level Six
Pelvic Muscle Tightening
With Breathing Patterns

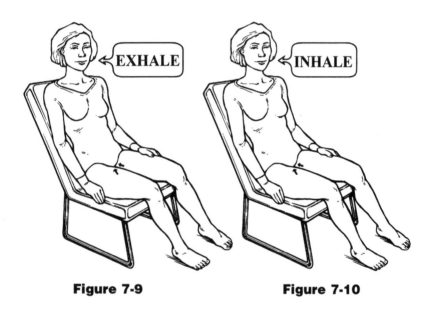

Figure 7-9   **Figure 7-10**

The breathing diaphragm and pelvic and urogenital diaphragms often contract and relax in a pattern with each other. This can lead to increased leaking with exercise or extensive coughing or sneezing. The following exercises are designed to separate action of the breathing diaphragm from the pelvic diaphragm muscles.

Exhale with Pelvic Muscle Tightening

First, focus on your natural breathing pattern. Notice that during inhalation the stomach rises slightly, and during exhalation the stomach falls. Once you feel the rhythm of your natural breathing, begin the exercise by tightening the pelvic muscles during exhalation, then releasing during inhalation (Fig.7-9). While exhaling, pull the pelvic muscles up and in, tightening the anal and urethral openings (and vaginal if appropriate) as you count slowly to 5. Then release and relax those muscles as you inhale for a slow count of 5.

Think or say, "Inhale, relax. Exhale, tighten." Do this gently and easily, practicing 2-3 times a day.

Inhale with Pelvic Muscle Tightening

First, focus on your natural breathing pattern. Notice that during inhalation the stomach rises slightly, and during exhalation the stomach falls. Once you feel the rhythm of your natural breathing, begin the exercise by tightening the pelvic muscles during inhalation then releasing during exhalation phase of breathing (Fig.7-10). While inhaling, pull the pelvic muscles up and in, tightening the anal and urethral openings (vaginal opening if appropriate) as you count slowly to 5. Then release and relax those muscles as you exhale for a slow count of 5.

Think or say, "Exhale, relax. Inhale, tighten." Do this gently and easily, practicing 2-3 times a day.

Level Seven
Pelvic Muscle Tightening During Coughing/Sneezing

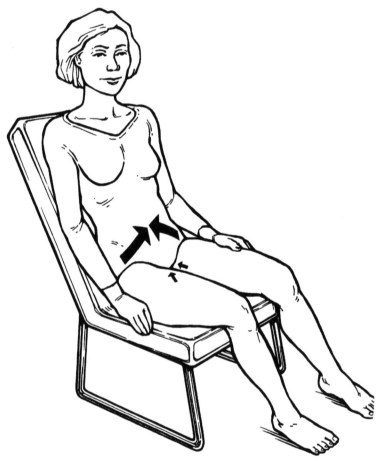

Figure 7-11

Lower Abdominals with
Pelvic Muscles

Step One: Actively exhale for a count of 5 while tightening the lower abdominal muscles (the muscles below the umbilicus). Then inhale and relax the abdominal muscles for a count of five.

Step Two: Actively exhale while tightening the lower abdominal muscles and pulling up and in with the pelvic muscles for a count of five. Then inhale and relax the abdominal muscles and pelvic muscles for a count of five.

Step Three: Tighten the lower abdominal and pelvic muscles while coughing or sneezing (Fig. 7-11).

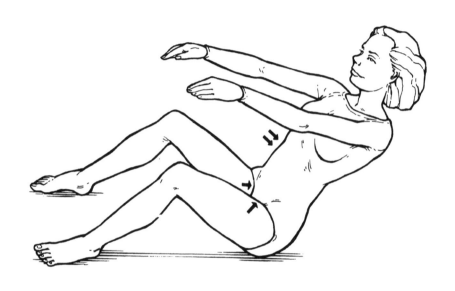

Figure 7-12

Upper Abdominals with Pelvic Muscles

Step One: Curl back from sitting (which tightens the upper abdominal muscles) while relaxing the pelvic muscles and exhaling for a count of five. Then return to the sit position and rest for a count of five.

Step Two: Curl back from sitting while tightening the pelvic muscles and exhaling for a count of five. Then return to the sit position while inhaling for a count of five.

Step Three: Curl back from sitting while tightening the pelvic muscles. Hold the position and cough or sneeze keeping the upper abdominal and pelvic muscles tight. This upper abdominal contraction helps to keep the force of the cough or sneeze in the upper abdomen rather than having the force transferred excessively to the pelvic region (Fig. 7-12).

Step Four: In a sitting position, tighten the upper abdominal and pelvic muscles, and while maintaining the contraction, sneeze or cough.

During coughing and sneezing, bracing with the upper abdominal muscles can protect the pelvic and bladder (detrusor) muscles from excessive forces.

Level Eight
Graded Pelvic Muscle Tightening: The Elevator

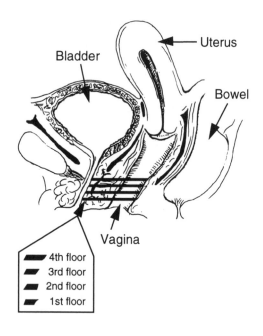

Figure 7-13

To perform this exercise think of an elevator going up one floor at a time. Pull up and in with the pelvic muscle group to the first floor, then the second floor, third floor, fourth floor, then to the penthouse (Fig.7-13). Pause momentarily at each floor, and move from one floor to another as smoothly as possible.

Now lower the elevator slowly from the penthouse to the fourth floor, third floor, second floor, first floor, then to the basement. Maintain your natural breathing pattern throughout this exercise. It will be easier to go up the elevator than down.

Practice a maximum of 1-3 repetitions. These exercises are termed concentric and eccentric contractions. The muscles fatigue quickly with this type of exercise.

CHAPTER 8

WHAT OTHER TECHNIQUES CAN HELP? PHYSIOLOGICAL QUIETING

AdjunctiveTechniques
Physiological Quieting

Individuals experiencing incontinence are often experiencing excessive arousal of the autonomic nervous system. Often the sympathetic or "fight or flight" portion of the autonomic nervous system is overactive. The result is an overactive bladder (detrusor) muscle that tells the brain it needs to empty too frequently.

Each individual responds to events in daily life through biochemical changes within the body and brain. The alarm in the morning is perceived by the ear, transferred to the brain center for hearing by biochemical events within the nerve, then interpreted by the brain centers which send messages to the rest of the body through additional chemicals saying, "open your eyes, jump out of bed, get dressed." The chemicals vary depending on how the event is perceived by the brain. If the event is perceived as an emergency, fight or flight event chemicals such as adrenaline and testosterone are released in increased amounts; if the event is perceived as normal and easy, the brain and body chemicals are different and give activating but calmer directions to all organs and tissues.

Some individuals with incontinence tend to have brains and nervous systems that respond to regular life events with fight or flight chemicals rather than quieting chemicals. The autonomic nervous system connections that control the bladder and bowel send out more fight or flight chemicals than quieting chemicals. We say it has a high idle at rest, always ready to jump into action. The on/off switch for full activation is hypersensitive. This means that even normal daily events may activate biochemicals that are meant only for use during short periods of high stress. Bladder muscle contractions, activated by the autonomic nervous system, result in frequent urges to urinate. Small amounts of urine are released when toileting so frequently, yet leaking of urine may still occur throughout the day or night.

It is important when treating incontinence to use management techniques that quiet the high idle or high resting level of the nervous system. It is important to use management techniques that assist the autonomic nervous system in responding to daily events with "calm" chemical activation of bladder and bowel instead of "fight or flight" activation.

These techniques are termed Physiological Quieting and include:

1) Diaphragmatic Breathing
2) Body/Mind Quieting

Diaphragmatic Breathing

The diaphragm is a large sheetlike muscle that rests in a dome shape upward into the chest cavity to the nipple area from the bottom of the ribcage and the lumbar spine. As you inhale the dome flattens and pulls down to the bottom of the ribcage. During exhale the diaphragm moves back to the dome shape. When breathing correctly, the shoulder and chest areas remain quiet, the jaw is relaxed, and the teeth are separated (Fig. 8-1). To practice:

"Inhale, let your abdomen rise. Exhale, let your abdomen fall. Quiet shoulders, quiet chest."

There is equal time for inhale and exhale. Inhale through the nose, exhale through the mouth or nose. Inhale is active while exhale is passive and quiet.

Practice diaphragmatic breathing initially in a reclined position, then in sitting and standing. Practice 4-5 diaphragmatic breaths every hour during the day.

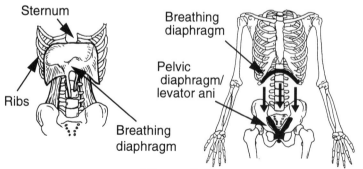

Figure 8-1

98

Body/Mind Quieting

Excessive bladder(detrusor) muscle resting tone and increased activity level of bladder and bowel contractions can be decreased through physiological quieting of the body and mind.

Find a quiet, warm room with a chair or bed that give complete support from your head to your feet. Use pillows for support of your neck, low back, arms, and knees where needed for comfort.

Then,

1) Focus on your breathing, feel the pattern of breathing, let your abdomen rise with inhale, fall with exhale.

2) Feel the support of the bed or chair and release into that support from the top of your head to the tips of your toes.

3) Focus on your face and neck. Notice where there is any tension or tightness, where there is quiet, calmness in each part of your face and neck. Then, say to yourself 3-4 times, "My face and neck muscles are quiet and calm, my face and neck muscles are calmer and calmer."

4) Proceed from head to toe in the same manner, focusing on each body part as you did the face and neck.

5) Focus again on diaphragmatic breathing.

One or two 20 minute body/mind quieting sessions a day are recommended. The Physiological Quieting audiotape is helpful to learn body/mind quieting.

CHAPTER 9

HOW DOES TREATMENT FOR STRESS AND URGE INCONTINENCE DIFFER?

Exercise Protocols Based on Type of Incontinence
Exercise protocols differ for each type of incontinence. They include:
1) Stress Incontinence Protocol
2) Urge Incontinence Protocol
3) Mixed Incontinence Protocol

Stress Incontinence Protocol includes:
1) Level One Exercise. Inhibit excessive resting tone of the pelvic and abdominal muscles through physiological quieting. This decreases excessive intra-abdominal pressure and assists the pelvic muscles in resting when appropriate and contracting quickly and intensely when needed.

2) Level Two and Four Exercises. Strengthen slow twitch fibers of the pelvic diaphragm/levator ani and obturator internus muscles to obtain optimal alignment of the bladder, bladder neck and urethra.

3) Level Three Exercise. Strengthen fast twitch fibers of the urogenital diaphragm muscles for quick response when coughing, sneezing or physical activity

that increases intra-abdominal pressure suddenly.

4) Level Five-Eight Exercises. Advanced techniques are appropriate on an individual basis.

Urge Incontinence Protocol includes:

1) Level One Exercise. This exercise improves the mind's connection to the bladder and pelvic muscle region. This exercise quiets the overactive bladder by decreasing intra-abdominal pressure, i.e., relaxed, toned abdominal muscles. It enables the individual to isolate pelvic muscle activity from abdominal and gluteal muscle contractions.

2) Level Three Exercise. Four to five quick contractions of the pelvic muscles when an individual feels an urge to toilet will quiet the overactive bladder muscle through a reflex arc that quiets the bladder when the pelvic muscles contract quickly.

3) Level Two and Four Exercises. Strengthen the pelvic diaphragm/levator ani muscles to obtain optimum position of bladder, bladder neck and urethra.

4) Adjunctive Techniques. Physiological quieting techniques quiet the sympathetic portion of the autonomic nervous system and the overactive bladder (detrusor) muscle.

5) Level Five-Eight Exercises. Advanced techniques are appropriate on an individual basis.

Mixed Incontinence Protocol includes:

The combination of exercises for stress and urge incontinence is effective for mixed incontinence symptoms.

CHAPTER 10

How Can Biofeedback Help With Exercise For Incontinence?

Biofeedback:
How can it help with exercises for incontinence?
By taking the guesswork out of doing a movement
that can't be seen.

Biofeedback measures and displays information occurring within the body, information about muscle tension (electrical activity of muscles), and breathing patterns. This is information a person normally does not perceive, information at an unconscious level. Biofeedback enables an individual to become aware of these processes at a conscious level.

Biofeedback is like a mirror: it shows the individual what the muscles are doing inside the body as they contract and relax. There are many muscles in the region that may be tightened when attempting to tighten the pelvic and urogenital diaphragm muscles. Biofeedback is a mirror that lets an individual separate one muscle group from the others. Just like the visual image in the mirror, biofeedback brings the image of muscle action to a screen so changes can be made quickly and accurately. If a woman wants to part her hair on the other side or put lipstick on her lips she uses the mirror to tell her first that it needs to be done and second that the changes she made are what she wants and where she wants them. Biofeedback tells the individual what the pelvic muscles are doing in isolation from other muscles, and it shows changes in the action of the muscles immediately and accurately as the individual tightens or relaxes them.

Biofeedback was first used to treat incontinence by Arnold Kegel, M.D., in the 1940s. He used a perineometer which measured pressure in the vaginal canal. The pressure increased when the pelvic muscles tightened and decreased when they relaxed. The original Kegel exercises were done using this method.

Today, biofeedback for urinary incontinence is a training method that gives quick, accurate information to the individual about pelvic muscle tightness and muscle relaxation via a monitor or a repetitive sound or a blinking light display. This immediate information improves learning new skills, such as tightening and relaxing pelvic muscles, because it helps the individual make immediate adjustments in the muscle activity depending on the desired action. Small sensors, connected to the biofeedback equipment, pick up and accurately measure activity of the pelvic muscles. This information is instantly transferred to the screen or display for the individual to see or hear.

Biofeedback for incontinence can provide information

about the pelvic and urogential diaphragm muscle groups. Pelvic muscle activity can be monitored directly through sensors recording the electrical activity at the nerve-muscle connection. This is called electromyography (EMG). The sensors are applied to the skin surface over the muscle group; or with internal vaginal or anal sensors, they are self-inserted in the vagina or anus to pick up pelvic muscle activity closer to the muscle surface. Surface sensors can also monitor abdominal, gluteal, adductor, and breathing diaphragm muscles.

Sensors pick up even slight contractions of the pelvic and urogential diaphragm muscles when the individual tries to tighten them, and the intensity and pattern of the contraction is visible immediately on the biofeedback display. A stronger contraction of the same muscles can be attempted and the observable difference between the two pictures is reinforcement for improved function of the pelvic muscles with each new contraction. As Martha said during her first biofeedback session, "Oh, so this is how it is supposed to feel when I do the exercise! I thought I was doing it right before but I wasn't using the right muscles." The guesswork is taken out of doing a movement that cannot be seen. The feel of the exercise is paired with the objective picture on the screen so changes are made more quickly. Problems with both stress and urge incontinence can be helped with this type of biofeedback.

The bladder (detrusor) muscle is not under our voluntary control, but an individual can learn to quiet the bladder's contractions through biofeedback that indirectly monitors the autonomic or "automatic" nervous system that controls the bladder. Although it is not possible to directly control the bladder, a general quieting of the autonomic nervous system will quiet the bladder since it receives its innervation from the autonomic nervous system. Because this nervous system controls breathing rate and circulation, if an individual learns to slow the breathing rate or warm the hands by increasing blood flow to the hands, there is a splash-over effect to the bladder. The bladder quiets so the frequent urge to urinate passes as the individual's breathing slows and hands warm. Sensors that pick up hand temperature tell the individual if the circulation is improving by showing the rising temperature on a monitor (for example from 86.5° to 88.7°). Sensors that measure movement of the diaphragm tell the individual how many breaths per minute occur, and how effectively the diaphragm is being used by showing diaphragm muscle activity increases and decreases on the monitor. Problems with urge incontinence, an unstable bladder, can be helped using this type of biofeedback.

Biofeedback can be used at home as well as in the clinic. Small home units are available that have their own small screens or attach to the monitor. The sensors are easy to use for the once-or-twice-a-day practice sessions. Some home units can "download" onto the clinic unit; that is, they store information about practice session frequency and results, which then is transferred to the clinic computer.

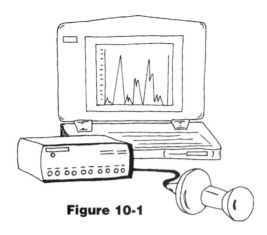

Figure 10-1

Biofeedback can be used successfully if an individual is able to process information through sight or sound and make modifications based on that input. The individual needs to be motivated to want to learn the exercise prescribed. There are no side effects and biofeedback is non-invasive.

Biofeedback in conjuction with therapeutic exercise has been shown to be more effective and faster in diminishing incontinence than exercise alone. Biofeedback gives more accurate, fast information to the brain which improves the learning curve, increases muscle strength more quickly, and reintegrates reflex arcs more completely.

CHAPTER 11
WHAT ARE SPECIAL CONSIDERATIONS FOR SPECIAL POPULATIONS?

Vulvodynia	Menopause
Interstitial Cystitis	Childhood Nocturnal Enuresis
Fibromyalgia	Prostatitis
Multiple Sclerosis	Benign Prostate Hyperplasia
Diabetes	Radical Prostatectomy
Pregnancy	

Vulvodynia

Vulvodynia symptoms include complaints of burning, stinging, and irritation of the vulva and labia of the female genitalia. Even light touch or pressure around the vaginal area causes severe pain which can make it difficult to wear any clothing, to sit in any positon, to ride a bicycle, to walk, or have intercourse. Urinating can cause extreme pain.

Treatment has included a low-oxalate diet, calcium citrate, an oxalate absorber, and glucosamine supplements.

Pelvic muscle exercises and biofeedback have been used successfully in cases of vulvodynia to increase pelvic muscle strength and decrease pain. Physio-logical quieting and diaphragmatic breathing are important components to decrease sympathetic nervous system activity and decrease pelvic muscle resting levels and muscle spasm. Pacing daily activities, alternating rest and work cycles, and changing nutritional habits are also important.

Interstitial Cystitis

Interstitial cystitis (IC) is a chronic inflammatory condition of the bladder with symptoms of severe frequency and urgency to urinate, suprapubic pressure, and pain. Toileting often occurs every 20-30 minutes during the day, therefore 8-16 times a day. Nocturia (frequent toileting at night) occurs as part of the syndrome. This can be as often as every hour and as infrequent as one to two times a night. Lower abdominal or suprapubic sensation can vary from infrequent discomfort to extreme pain. Pain can also be in the low back, vaginal, and inner thigh regions. Sleep is signif-icantly disrupted since toileting is so frequent, and therefore fatique is a significant side effect. Leaking often occurs in conjunction with the urgency and frequency symptoms. Exacerbations may occur with intercourse or menstrual cycle.

Diagnosis is made by excluding other disorders, and is often verified by cystoscopic findings of diffuse hemorragic (bleeding or oozing) spots on the bladder lining. Interstitial cystitis is of unkown origin and may have several causes.

Treatment has included low dose tricyclic anti-depressant medications (10-75 mg). DMSO cocktail instilled in the bladder weekly for 6-20 weeks has decreased symptoms in some individuals. Hydrodistension of the bladder (stretching the bladder using an infusion of water) is done under anesthesia and has alleviated symptoms in some cases. Bladder surgery is considered in some intractable situations.

Myofascial release, cranial sacral therapy, and trigger point massage can relieve pain and trigger point symptoms. Electrical stimulation can also help with relief of muscle trigger points and muscle hyperactivity.

Pelvic muscle exercises with biofeedback have been helpful in relieving symptoms of interstitial cystitis. Contracting/relaxing the pelvic muscles increases circulation to nerves and muscles of the region and can help normalize the numerous reflex arcs that coordinate the bladder and bowel system. Pelvic muscle exercise increases muscle strength and improves muscle function.

Physiological quieting with biofeedback has helped to relieve symptoms by quieting or inhibiting excessive bladder contractions and helping the pelvic muscles to relax in the resting state.

Dietary changes have also helped some individuals with IC. Avoiding acidic and spicy food and drink has alleviated some symptoms. Eliminating caffeine and consuming 6-8 glasses of fluid a day have been important dietary changes. Any constipation or other bowel problems need to be addressed through dietary changes and exercise because the bowel is integrally connected to the bladder, and any distension or irritation of the bowel causes irritation of the bladder.

Electrical stimulation intravaginally has also assisted in quieting or inhibiting the overactive bladder muscle. Individuals report decreased suprapubic and back pain as well as less frequent toileting episodes.

Fibromyalgia

Fibromyalgia is described as widespread pain of more than three months duration in combination with tenderness of specific sites throughout the body. Tenderness can vary from a grimace or flinch to intolerable pain from light touch. Specific complaints often include urinary frequency, lower abdominal pain and pressure, leaking, enuresis, and interstitial cystitis-like symptoms.

Pelvic muscle exercises, physiological quieting, diaphragmatic breathing, and biofeedback are important components of treatment for fibromyalgia and incontinence. Medication, often tricyclic antidepressents, can be an important component of treatment to gain long-term supression of leaking.

Multiple Sclerosis

Multiple sclerosis (MS) is a neurological disorder affecting sensation, body movement, and function. Plaque formation on nerves throughout the brain and peripheral nervous system acts as a blockade to normal nerve transmission. The plaques may change in location and severity with time so symptoms change too.

Plaques on nerves affecting the bowel and bladder are relatively common in MS. Ten percent of the time, bladder symptoms are the initial symptoms leading to the MS diagnosis. Common symptoms often include urinary urgency and frequency; difficulty initiating urination; small, weak stream flow; lack of complete bladder emptying; nighttime leaking; and inability to know when to toilet.

If the plaque is affecting nerves that innervate the pelvic muscles, the symptoms may be: a) leaking of urine because the muscles are too weak or slow in reacting to hold urine in, or b) difficulty releasing the muscles to let all the urine flow out. Joan described that, despite her urge to go to the toilet, she had to concentrate on relaxing the pelvic muscles as she sat on the toilet so she could initiate a good stream of urine even though she had the urge to go to the toilet.

If the plaque is affecting the nerves that innervate the bladder and urethra, the bladder may be floppy and unable to contract enough to push the urine out, and/or the internal sphincter may tighten excessively so the urine cannot flow down the urethra. This is called bladder-sphincter dysenergia. The result is retention of urine in the bladder and overflow incontinence or leaking at unpredictable times.

Medication, often hytrin, is one of the first recommendations for treatment. It has the effect of increasing action of the bladder muscle and relaxing the internal sphincter muscle.

Physiological quieting with diaphragmatic breathing

can assist in relaxing the pelvic muscles and normalizing autonomic nervous system messages to the bladder and urethra.

Pelvic muscle exercises can be an important treatment as long as there is an understanding that the rest phase of exercise is as important as the contract phase. Exercise improves circulation and stimulates nerve muscle connections. Because fatigue is a factor in MS, short periods of exercise (3-5 minutes) are recommended.

Diabetes

Diabetes is a metabolic condition characterized by the body's inability to adequately produce and/or effectively utilize insulin. This affects every body organ in some way. The urinary consequences can include frequency and urgency of urination when blood sugars are elevated. Peripheral neuropathy can result in an atonic, floppy, bladder that is unable to empty completely. Sensation can also be affected, so messages about the need to urinate are not always accurately communicated to the brain. Pelvic muscle weakness due to neuropathy and inadequate circulation can lead to leaking during daily physical activities. Excessive sugar in the urine causes bladder irritation resulting in frequent urge sensations when there is not a full bladder.

The most important treatment for bladder symptoms in diabetes is maintenance of good control of blood sugar levels through medication, regular exercise, a diet low in sugar and protein, and regular blood glucose monitoring.

The Beyond Kegel Exercise Protocol can be very beneficial to re-educate the pelvic and urogential diaphragm muscles and normalize the bladder muscle function if the diabetes control is good. A maintenance level of exercise is usually 5-10 minutes daily.

Physiological quieting is beneficial in blood glucose regulation and in bladder function, so a 20 minute session once a day is recommended.

Pregnancy

The anatomical and physiological changes during pregnancy predispose the woman to incontinence episodes during or after childbirth. As pregnancy progresses, the uterus enlarges to accommodate the growing fetus and this puts pressure on the bladder. The ligamentous and fascial supportive structures relax during pregnancy to allow the uterus to grow and to enable the pelvis to expand for a vaginal delivery. Secondarily, the ligaments and fascia cannot support the bladder and bladder angle as effectively. Constipation is often a problem in the last trimester (3months) of pregnancy due to the crowded conditions in the pelvis and the physiological change in contractility of the lower bowel. Constipation causes increased irritation of the bladder which can precipitate leaking.

During childbirth, the pudendal nerve, that innervates the pelvic muscles, can be traumatized so there is dysfunction of the muscle-nerve connection. The pelvic muscles are stretched and sometimes injured during the delivery process. Relaxation of the ligamentous and fascial structures continues for several months after the delivery or until breastfeeding ceases. The structures of the lower pelvis, bladder, uterus, and bowel usually return to the prepregnancy state gradually over several months. During this time of recovery some women experience leaking.

It is common for women to be taught Kegel exercises for the purpose of supporting the growing uterus and preparing for delivery. The recommendations for exercise of the pelvic muscles during pregnancy include:

Level One Exercise
Relaxed Awareness of the Pelvic Muscles
Level Two Exercise
Assisted Pelvic Muscle Tightening using
Obturator Internus and Adductor Muscles
Level Four Exercise
Quick Contractions of Urogenital Diaphragm
Adjunctive Techniques
Physiological Quieting and Diaphragmatic
Breathing

Relaxed Awareness of the Pelvic Muscles develops the body/mind connection, begins the awarenenss of the individual's breathing rhythm, and separates the pelvic muscle action from the other muscles of the body. It is the essential first step to begin each exercise session even though it takes only a few minutes to accomplish.

Assisted Pelvic Muscle Tightening Using Obturator Internus Muscles provides optimum support for the internal organs of bowel, uterus, and bladder with increased tone of the pelvic diaphragm and obturator internus muscles. These are predominantly slow twitch fibers for postural support of those internal organs. Five to seven minutes of practice twice a day is recommended. Practice in supine/reclining, sitting, and standing positions.

Quick Contractions of the Urogenital Diaphragm Muscles provides the explosive speed and strength of the fast twitch fiber contractions when a cough, sneeze, etc. requires a quick response of the urogenital diaphragm and external sphincter muscles to stop urine from leaking. Practice 5-10 repetitions before and after each Level Two exercise set.

Physiological quieting and diaphragmatic breathing are important for general health and stress reduction during pregnancy and postpartum. They enable active participation of the woman during delivery. Physiological quieting enables the woman to maintain efficient, quiet activity of all systems while the uterus does its work of delivering the baby. Diaphragmatic breathing maintains adequate oxygen flow to the mother and baby and is a primary tool in pain control and stress reduction during delivery. Twenty minutes a day of practice is recommended. The Physiological Quieting audiotape is available through Phoenix Publishing.

During the delivery process, the woman assists by bearing down or pushing to help the fetus descend into the birth canal. The most efficient method to accomplish this involves a coordination of voluntary activity between the abdominal, breathing diaphragm, and

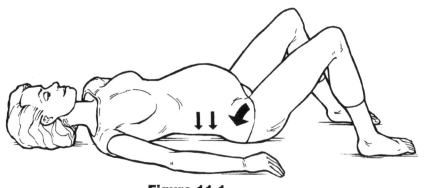

Figure 11-1

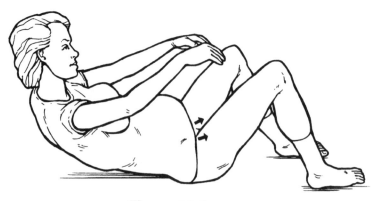

Figure 11-2

116

pelvic muscles.

During delivery, the pelvic musculature must be as relaxed as possible so that as the fetus descends, it is not hitting a "brick wall." At the same time, the abdominals are tightening and the breathing diaphragm is set in the descended position to increase intra-abdominal pressure to help with pushing the fetus down the birth canal. At any other time during activities of daily living, if there is increased intra-abdominal pressure with abdominal tightening, the desire is to tighten the pelvic muscles, but during childbirth, it is important they relax.

To learn this coordindated sequence of muscle activity for delivery, the Three-in-One Exercise should be practiced:

1) Recline on your back, knees bent, feet flat on the floor. Inhale, setting the breathing diaphragm in the descended or lowered position as you pos-teriorly tilt your pelvis using the abdominal muscles (Fig. 11-1).

2) Relax, the pelvic muscles.

3) Curl up, bringing your head and shoulders off the surface as you exhale. Hold for a slow count of 5-10. Then relax into the start position (Fig. 11-2).

Repeat this exercise 4-5 times daily during the last 3 months of pregnancy.

During delivery, the Three-in-One sequence is done during the pushing phase, whether in sitting, squatting or side lying.

After delivery, the Three-in-One Exercise is modified so that pelvic muscle tightening instead of relaxing is performed in step two of the exercise. Progress from 4-5 repetitions up to 15-20 repetitions of this exercise over a 4-6 week period after delivering.

Menopause

When a woman ceases menstruating, other physical changes associated with hormonal changes, primarily estrogen depletion, occur. The pelvic muscles, connective tissue, fascia, and ligaments are estrogen dependent. As estrogen decreases with menopause, the pelvic tissues become dry, thin, and less elastic. The bladder and bladder neck become more mobile as the supportive structures relax and thin. The bladder becomes more irritable. The result can be urge and/or stress incontinence. It is common for women in this age group to gain some weight and even a five-pound weight gain may increase the incidence of incontinence.

Incontinence in this age group is most often treated conservatively with exercise and medication after a medical evaluation. The Beyond Kegel Exercise Protocol performed 7-10 minutes daily is recommended as a preventive exercise program for women after the age of 40 to maintain pelvic muscle strength and bladder support. Physiological quieting, 20 minutes daily, helps normalize bladder muscle activity so urge sensations are decreased. Moderate weightbearing, aerobic exercise, 30 minutes daily, helps maintain bone strength and heart/lung health.

Nocturnal Enuresis in Children
Nighttime Wetting

Children are usually dry at night between the ages of 3 and 4. After 8 years old, frequent leaking is considered abnormal, but in reality it is relatively common; approximately five percent of 10 year olds and 1 to 2 percent of adults still leak at night. Twice as many boys experience the problem as do girls. Nocturnal enuresis tends to run in families. It is unusual for nighttime wetting in children to be due to medical problems, but there should be a check for urinary tract infection, diabetes, or an anatomical abnormality. Nighttime wetting can also result from emotional trauma, such as separation from a parent or abuse, but most of the time it is not a psychologically caused problem. Some children have a small bladder capacity and may be helped by a high fluid intake and bladder training (to wait before urinating for increasing periods of time).

In general, nocturnal enuresis in children can be regarded as the need to learn a developmental skill that did not come automatically for these children, and for the pelvic muscles and bladder muscle to mature in tone and coordination in order to function at a more sophisticated level at night as well as during the day.

Bedwetting will often cause increased tension in the family. Someone or something is sometimes blamed for the behavior. The child, as well as the rest of the family, needs to understand that bedwetting is not usually intentional; and is not a result of laziness or not caring. In most cases, if parents are calm and patient,

the problem can be effectively treated.
Treatment includes

1) Exercises to strengthen and tone the pelvic muscles
2) Exercises to quiet the bladder muscle
3) Behavioral techniques to train awakening at night to toilet
4) Drinking behavior for adequate fluid intake

Exercises to strengthen and tone the pelvic muscles include:

a. Leg squeezes with pelvic muscle tightening. The position to start this exercise in is reclined on the bed or floor with hips and knees bent and feet resting on the supporting surface. Place a 7-9 inch soft ball between the knees. The instructions are, "Squeeze the ball between your knees and tighten the pelvic muscles as if you were going to stop a bowel movement. Hold while counting out loud to 10. Then relax your knees and pelvic muscles and rest for a count of 10." To make it more fun, count elephants, dinosaurs, etc. "One elephant, two elephant......" (Fig.11-3)

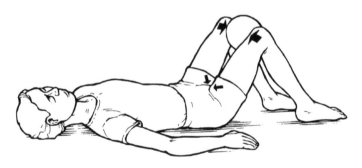

Figure 11-3

b. Hip bridges with pelvic muscle tightening. The position to start this exercise in is reclined on the bed or floor with hips and knees bent and feet resting on the supporting surface. The instructions are, "Lift your hips off the supporting surface and hold the position as you pull the pelvic muscles up and in as if you were going to stop a bowel movement or stop urinating. Hold while counting out loud to 10. Then return to the rest position for a count of 10." To make it more fun, count boats, fish, or alligators that go under the bridge. "One alligator, two alligator......." (Fig.11-4)

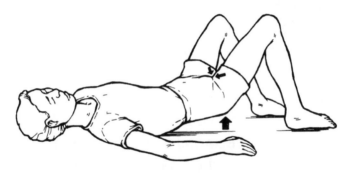

Figure 11-4

These exercises are done two times a day, morning and evening, 10 repetitions of each exercise.

Exercises to quiet the bladder muscle
   1) Physiological quieting- hand warming
   2) Physiological quieting- diaphragmatic breathing

Physiological quieting—hand warming: Given a small thermometer or a mood ring or card, the child has fun increasing the temperature on the thermometer or changing the color on the mood ring or card. As the temperature increases in the hands, the nervous system controlling that also quiets the bladder muscle so it doesn't contract as quickly, telling the brain it has to go to the toilet. The instructions are to think five times slowly, "My hands are warmer and warmer." Then, "Think of the warmest place to put your hands and feel the warmth from that place warming your hands, warmer and warmer."

Physiological quieting—diaphragmatic breathing: This is also called belly button breathing because as the child breathes, the belly button moves up and down. First, have the child try the exercise reclined on the back with the head supported on a small pillow. A small book or the child's hand is placed on the tummy over the belly button. Then the instructions are, "As you breathe in, let your belly button rise," and, "As you breathe out, let your belly button fall," and "See and feel your hand move up and down with your breathing." The second step is, "Let your belly button rise for a slow count of four as you breathe in. Then let your belly button fall for a slow count of four as you breathe out."

These exercises are practiced two to three times a day for 60-90 seconds each. It is important for the child to practice each of these exercises at bedtime.

Behavioral techniques to train awakening at night to toilet
Parents often try to cure bedwetting by carrying the sleeping child to the toilet when the parents go to bed. This may prevent wetting, but it does not help the child

to have independent control. It is essential that the child awaken and make the connection between waking and the desire to urinate. An enuresis alarm and a star chart enables the child to learn this skill in a positive way. The enuresis alarm is a small buzzer that velcros on the pajama at shoulder level. It is connected to a small sensor that is attached in the underpants. When even a small amount of urine touches the sensor, the buzzer sounds, waking the child. The child has been instructed to get up and go to the toilet when the buzzer sounds. Dry pants are in the bathroom. After toileting and changing pants, the child returns to bed and sleep. A gold star is placed on a chart if the child goes through the night without wetting. A silver star is placed on the chart if the child gets up to the buzzer, toilets, and changes wet underwear. No comments or "bad marks" are given for wet nights. When an entire week is "dry," the child is rewarded with a special treat.

The child is shown how to take care of wet under-wear and sheets. Depending on the age, a child can be shown to place them in a covered laundry bin or to place them in the washer and wash them. Acknowledging the problem and planning the necessary steps to deal with it is important in taking the blame and shame away from nighttime wetting.

Drinking behavior for adequate fluid intake

One of the first things parents and children commonly do to "cure" night- time wetting is to decrease the amount of fluid the child is consuming.

The result is that the bladder (detrusor) muscle "shrinks" and can hold less and less before it lets the brain know it is time to urinate. This decrease in fluid intake also causes more concentrated waste products in the urine which is irritating to the bladder lining. Decreased fluid intake can cause dehydration which affects all body functions. Instead of limiting fluids, the child should drink 4-6 eight-ounce glasses of appropriate fluid a day. Appropriate fluids include water, fruit juice, and milk. Caffeine is irritating to the bladder and the nervous system, so colas, coffee, and tea are not recommended. If the child drinks eight ounces of fluid with each meal, and a small bike bottle of fluid between meals, the amount is adequate.

The equipment needed for this program is relatively simple and easy to obtain. The bike bottle and ball can be purchased in any grocery or convenience store. The child loves to pick out the most colorful ball or the bottle with the current popular theme printed on it. The enuresis alarm and star chart can be purchased through a medical supply store.

The program usually takes between 2-6 weeks. It has been noted that enuresis may reoccur months or years after the "cure," when the child has undergone a growth spurt or has had the flu or other systemic illness. If this happens, a "refresher course" of 1-2 weeks of exercise and enuresis alarm is usually adequate to return to normal.

Prostate Enlargement
Benign Prostate Hyperplasia
Radical Prostatectomy
Prostatitis

Urinary incontinence in men is usually experienced after age 60 and often is related to prostate enlargement, whether benign or cancerous.

The Prostate Gland

The male prostrate gland surrounds the urethra just below the bladder outlet. It has been compared to an apple with the urethra being the core (Fig.11-5). The prostate gland is composed of: (1) glands that produce fluid to carry the sperm through the urethra and out, (2) muscle that contracts during ejaculation to propel the semen through the urethra to the outside environment, and (3) fibrous or connective tissue, a portion of which forms a firm outer shell that protects the pulpy inner core (Fig.11-6).

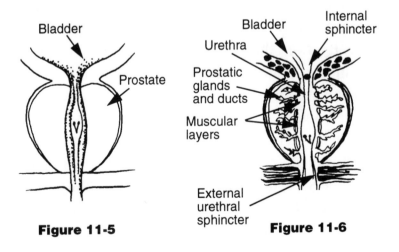

Figure 11-5

Figure 11-6

At puberty, the prostate is about the size of a walnut. After 40, the prostate in most men, gradually becomes enlarged, probably in response to the changing levels of the male hormone testosterone. This growth may cause incontinence problems, including leaking with exertion, frequency of urination, incomplete emptying of the bladder, and/or weak urine flow.

Men have several mechanisms to prevent leaking. Between the bladder outlet and the prostate is the internal sphincter muscle that automatically contracts or closes to keep urine in the bladder and relaxes to release it. The external sphincter muscle is located just below the prostate gland and performs the same function. It is under the individual's voluntary control. The prostate gland supports the urethra and both have muscular layers, so together they contract or tighten to stop urine flow or relax/release to facilitate the flow of urine outward.

Symptoms

As the prostate enlarges, it can occlude or block the urethra so urine cannot flow out effectively and efficiently, even though the bladder may be contracting to push the urine out and the internal and external sphincter muscles are relaxed to release urine. When this obstruction occurs, the symptoms can include a weak stream of urine, frequent feelings of urge to urinate but only small amounts of urine are released, relatively small leaks of urine during physical activity, and/or occasional large leaking episodes when there is the urge to toilet and it has been several hours since the last toileting and/or a considerable fluid intake.

Urethral blockage by the prostate can cause incomplete emptying of the bladder. The medical term for this is post void residual (PVR). This can lead to a bladder infection, irritated bladder lining, or urine reflux into the kidneys.

Prostatitis

Prostatitis is acute or chronic bacterial or non-bacterial caused pain in the epdidymis in male genitalia. Pelvic muscle exercises and biofeedback can be an important treatment component to increase circulation and decrease pelvic muscle tone in prostatitis. During pelvic muscle exercise there is an emphasis on the rest phase of contract/relax activity.

Benign Prostate Hyperplasia

Prostate enlargement can be benign/nonmalignant or cancerous. If it is benign, a transurethral prostatectomy (TURP) can be performed to remove the excess tissue that is blocking the urethra. It is termed by some the "roto rooter" method of cleaning out the prostate problem. A long tube is placed through the urethra and into the bladder. Like a cystoscope, the miniature camera within the tube can inspect the urethra and bladder. When the excess prostate tissue is located, another device is used through the tube to remove the tissue. The surgery takes about one hour and the individual may be in the hospital 2-3 days. A result of this surgery can be total or partial urinary incontinence.

Balloon urethroplasty (balloon dilation of the urethra) and transurethral hyperthermia, using microwave radiation, are also possibilities in treating prostate enlargement that is obstructing urine flow through the urethra. As indicated in the chapter on medications, there are several alpha adrenergic agents that may prove helpful.

Radical Prostatectomy

In cancerous enlargement of the prostate gland, radical prostatectomy is often recommended. This is complete removal of the prostate gland and related tissue in the hope of eliminating all cancerous cells. In some cases, pelvic lymph nodes are also removed. Other treatment options include chemotherapy, radiation therapy, and hormonal therapy including removal of the testicles to eliminate testosterone. A result of these treatment approaches can be total or partial urinary incontinence.

Infections of the bladder and prostate can lead to urinary incontinence in men. Infections are treated with antibiotics. Bladder masses, neurologic conditions, and constipation can also precipitate leaking.

Treatment for Incontinence
Exercise

The first line of treatment for urinary incontinence in men is usually medication and exercise. The exercises described in this book are appropriate for men and their effectiveness will improve with some modifications.

There is a tendency for men who experience leaking to tighten every muscle in the pelvic area in an attempt to stop the involuntary flow of urine. They tighten the buttocks, pelvic muscles, external anal sphincter, and abdominal muscles in a chronic maximal contraction. These muscles eventually fatigue and even more leaking occurs. The first step in gaining continence for men is learning to relax the muscles completely. The second step is learning to contract/tighten only the appropriate muscles while leaving the others relaxed. Contraction of the appropriate muscles, the pelvic diaphragm, urethral diaphragm, and external sphincter muscles, is often most effective at a submaximal or easy contraction. Then the individual gradually builds up to a maximal contraction of the appropriate muscles. Biofeedback is very effective in helping the individual learn how to isolate appropriate muscles, completely relax them, and contract muscles to effective intensities.

Men often orient the pelvic floor contraction to the anal area rather than the urethral or penis portion of the muscular hammock. To orient the contractions towards the urethral area, have the individual place his hands on the lower abdomen/symphysis pubis area and contract towards the finger tips. Another technique involves contracting the pelvic muscles to make the penis move up and down a quarter to one-half inch.

Treatment duration for men who have had radical prostatectomies and radiation may be longer than the typical incontinence treatment program of 4-8 weeks of exercise. Improvement has been noted over a 12-month exercise program, possibly due to nerve and muscle regeneration and healing. Once the exercise progression is completed (usually in 4-6 weeks), the individual is seen once every 4-8 weeks for follow- up and alterations to the program. An important aspect of the follow-up visits with these individuals is encouragement to continue the regular exercise protocol, fluid intake, and lifestyle changes.

A general exercise program of walking, hiking, swimming, etc. is recommended for 30-60 minutes daily at a moderate level of exertion. A general exercise program optimizes all organ system functions; increases metabolism; and optimizes hormonal levels, including hormones that affect mood and energy levels.

Men will ask if the exercises can improve impotence if that has been a result of surgery or radiation. There are no objective findings to indicate that exercise can reverse this problem, but the stimulation to all body systems, including circulatory, hormonal, and neuro-logical, can only be positive for the body healing itself.

Nutrition

One of the first actions often taken by men experiencing urinary incontinence is to decrease fluid intake throughout the day and night. The immediate result of this may be a little less leaking but the long term result can be devastating. Less fluid in the bladder causes the bladder to shrink because it responds to the volume of liquid by adjusting in size much like a balloon enlarges as it is filled with air. A smaller bladder means it sends more frequent messages to the brain that it needs to empty. Eventually the individual can be toileting every 30 minutes during the day and hourly at night.

Less urine means the urine is more concentrated and often more irritating to the bladder lining. This can cause the bladder to contract more frequently and strongly, so some men describe experiencing an explosion of urine they cannot control. Concentrated urine can lead to bladder and lower abdominal discomfort and even bladder infections.

It is important that 6-8 glasses of non-caffeinated fluid be consumed daily. It is appropriate to stop fluids after 6:00 p.m. to facilitate longer periods between toileting during the night. The fluid intake is best if it is spread out evenly through the day.

Protection

Men comment that they do not go out socially or they curtail physical activity because they fear leaking will be obvious due to staining or odor. Appropriate pads can alleviate these fears. Adhesive backed pads attach to underwear. Disposable undergarments are available through the mail or in grocery stores or pharmacies. Some men will tell of innovative approaches to absorbing leaks, including toilet paper or a soft washcloth in a baggie surrounding the penis. Penis clamps can be used for short periods but are not appropriate for day-long use. Intermittent catheterization is often the most appropriate method if there is a high PVR. The catheterization can empty the bladder effectively and provide a period of time with no leaking.

CHAPTER 12
WHAT MEDICATIONS CAN HELP?

Medications have been shown to be beneficial in treating urinary incontinence. In conjunction with exercise and behavioral strategies, they are recommended as the first step in treating incontinence in the Clinical Practice Guideline published by the Department of Health and Human Services, 1996.

Short term medication trials benefit some patients with urge incontinence, but the side effects can be significant and research indicates that few individuals become symptom-free.

Medication use may improve symptoms in approximately half of the individuals with stress or mixed incontinence, but again few become symptom-free. Medications used for stress incontinence have fewer side effects than those used for urge incontinence.

Medications used for overflow incontinence exhibit significant side effects, and improvement in symptoms varies.

Medication use should be based on individual patient needs, ie., contraindications, cost, and drug interactions. Initial dosages in most medications used for incontinence should be low and increased slowly.

Pharmacologic treatment for urinary incontinence is an important component of treatment but needs to be used in combination with exercise, behavioral and sometimes surgical strategies.

Medications Used to Relieve Incontinence
Urge Incontinence
Anticholinergic Agents
   oxybutynin (Ditropan)
   dicyclomine hydrochloride (Bentyl)
   propantheline (Pro-Banthine)
   hyoscyamine (Levsin)
Estrogen Replacement Therapy (ERT)
Tricyclic Antidepressant Agents
   imipramine (Tofranil)
   doxepin (Sinequan)
   desipramine (Norpramin)
   nortriptyline (Pamelor)
   amitriptyline (Elavil)

Stress Incontinence
Alpha Adrenergic Agonists
   phenylpropanolamine (PPA)
Estrogen Replacement Therapy (ERT)
Combination Therapy
   tricyclic antidepressent agents
   and antidiuretic hormone

Overflow Incontinence
Alpha Adrenergic Antagonists
   terazosin (Hytrin)
   prazosin (Minipress)
   doxazosin (Cardura)
Cholinergic Agonists
   bethanechol (Urecholine)

Description of Commonly Used Medications
Urge Incontinence
Anticholinergic Agents

Function: Decreases bladder contractions, relaxes smooth muscle

Effect: Decreases urge incontinence leaking, increases bladder capacity, increases time between voiding

Examples:	Dose
oxybutynin (Ditropan)	2.5-5 mg 1-4x/day
propantheline (Pro-Banthine)	7.5-30 mg, 15-60mg
dicyclomine hydrochloride (Bentyl)	20 mg 4x/day
hyoscyamine (Levsin)	0.125-0.25 mg 3-4 x/day

Side effects: Dry skin, blurred vision, change in mental state, drowsiness, confusion, nausea, constipation, dry mouth, tachycardia (increased heart rate), weakness, orthostatic hypotension (low blood pressure on arising from reclining)

Note: Should not be used if narrow angle glaucoma is present.

Estrogen Replacement Therapy (ERT)

Tricyclic Antidepressant Agents (TCA)

Function: Increases CNS serotonin neurotransmitter levels

Effect: Reduces daytime leaking, reduces nighttime leaking

Examples	Dose
imipramine (Tofranil)	10-25 mg 1-4x/day
doxepin (Sinequan)	10-50 mg 3x/day
desipramine (Norpramin)	25 mg 1-3x/day
nortriptyline (Pamelor)	10-25 mg 1-3x/day
amitriptyline (Elavil)	10-25 mg 3-4x/day

Side effects: cardiac alterations, anticholinergic effects, fatigue, xerostomia, dizziness, blurred vision

Stress Incontinence

Alpha Adrenergic Agonists

Function: Affects receptors at bladder neck, internal sphincter, and proximal urethra causing muscle contraction in this area

Effect: Decreases leaking with intra-abdominal pressure, tightens bladder outlet muscle

Examples	Dose
phenylpropanolamine (PPA) (Dexatrim)	25-50 mg 4x/day
psuedoephedrine (Sudafed)	30-60 mg 4x/day

Side Effects: Nausea, xerostomia, insomnia, restlessness, anxiety, headache, hypertension, heart palpitations

Note: Not to be used in people with increased blood pressure/hypertension, severe congestive heart failure, cardiac arrhythmias

Estrogen Replacement Therapy(ERT)

Function: Restore urethral mucosa, increase vascularity, tone and responsiveness of urethral muscle, increase alpha adrenergic receptors of urethra

Effect: Improve internal sphincter function, decrease incontinence with increased intra-abdominal pressure, decreases irritative voiding symptoms, decreases frequency of urination especially at night

Examples	Dose
conjugated estrogen (Premarin)	0.623-1.25 mg daily

Side Effects: Not recommended for women with a history of breast or uterine cancer, blood clots, or liver damage

Combination Therapy- ERT and PPA

Recommended in stress incontinence in postmenopausal women if single drug therapy has proven inadequate

Tricyclic Antidepressant Agents
    imipramine (Tofranil)   75 mg/day
    (See description under Urge Incontinence medications.)
    (Propranolol and other beta blockers are not recommended at this time due to lack of clinical research.)

Antidiurectic Hormone
    desmopressin (DDAVP)
    Effect: Decreases nocturnal enuresis (nighttime wetting) and nighttime polyuria; at this time used for children only

Overflow Incontinence
    Alpha Adrenergic Antagonists
    Function: Relaxes internal sphincter muscle
    Effect: Increases outlet size causing improved flow of urine, decreased residual urine, decreased leaking due to more complete emptying

Examples	*Dose*
terazosin (Hytrin)	1 mg daily
prazosin (Minipress)	1 mg 2-3x/daily
doxazosin (Cardura)	1 mg daily

    Side Effects: Orthostatic hypotension (which can lead to falls, should be taken at bedtime), tachycardia (increased heart rate)

Cholinergic Agonists
    Function: Increases bladder muscle contractions
    Effect: Increases force with which bladder muscle pushes urine down and out the urethra, decreases residual urine, decreases leaking because of more complete emptying

Example   *Dose*
bethanechol (Urecholine)   10-50 mg 2-4x/day
Side Effects: flushing, abdominal cramps, diarrhea,
nausea and vomiting, sweating, salivation

Medications that Cause Incontinence Symptoms

Many of the same medications used to treat incontinence can also cause incontinence if used inappropriately. Medications used to treat other conditions can have side effects that cause incontinence.

Medication	Possible Side Effects
Sedatives/Hypnotics	sedation, immobility, muscle relaxation,
CNS Depressants diazepan (Valium) flurazepam (Dalmane) alcohol	delirium, frequency and uregency leaking
Diuretics furosemide (Lasix) bumetanide (Bumex) loop diuretics	polyuria, frequency and urgency leaking
Antipsychotics thioridazine (Mellaril) haloperidol (Haldol)	sedation, rigidity, immobility, urge and overflow leaking, anticholinergic actions
Antidepressants imiprimine (Tofranil) doxepin (Sinequan) desipramine (Norpramin) amitriptyline (Elavil)	fatique, dizziness, bladder relaxation, constipation
Anti-Parkinson Agents benztropine (Cogentin) trihexyphenidyl (Artane)	bladder relaxation, urge and overflow leaking

Anticholinergic Agents antihistamines— diphenhydramine (Benadryl) hydroxyzine (Vistaril, Atarax)	sedation, urine retention, weak stream, frequency, urge and overflow leaking, fecal impaction
Alpha Adrenergic Agonist Agents phenylpropranolamine (Ephedrine)	sedation, urine retention, weak stream, frequency, urge and overflow leaking
Alpha Adrenergic Antagonist Agents prazosin (Minipress) terazosin (Hytrin) doxazosin (Cardura)	urethral relaxation, leak with cough/ sneeze/laugh
Calcium Channel Blocking Agents nifedipine (Adalat, Procardia) diltiazem (Cardizem)	urine retention, fluid retention, bladder (detrusor) relaxation
Narcotic Analgesic Agents morphine, etc.	urine retention, sedation, delirium fecal impaction
Antihypertensive Agents	bladder and sphincter relaxation
Caffeine	aggravation or precipitation of leaking

CHAPTER 13

How Did Exercise Help?

Case Studies
What Did Exercise Do To Help?

Remember the case studies at the beginning of this book in Chapter 3? Go back now, review the histories and outline the recommendations you would have for each individual to become continent and/or resume regular daily acitivities.

What lifestyle changes would you recommend?

What exercises and adjunctive techniques of physiological quieting will help them and why?

How often should they do the exercises and adjunctive techniques?

What is success?

Then, read this chapter to see how each individual took back the control of incontinence and returned to a fullfilling daily life.

Lizzie, 9 years old: Bedwetting

Lizzie, 9 years old, was seen for 3 visits over a 6-week period. She carried out the nocturnal enuresis exercise and alarm protocol. Within 3 weeks she was dry at night.

She has been followed for 3 years. There has been a return of symptoms once after a growth spurt. She went back on the program for 2 weeks and has been dry since then.

Mary, 29 years old: Stress Incontinence

Mary, 29 years old, was seen for 10 visits over a 4-month period of time. Exercises prescribed included the Beyond Kegels Exercise Protocol for incontinence and lumbar stabilization exercises for low back pain. Life style changes were also a major emphasis in her treatment program. Initially she began a paced aerobic exercise program, 30 minutes daily followed by lumbar stabilization exercises and a rest period of 30 minutes. She changed her work schedule to two three-hour work shifts instead of 6 continuous hours of work. Between the 3 hour shifts, she did her exercise, rested, and ate lunch which she used to skip.

Three weeks after beginning the exercise and lifestyle change protocol, Mary was toileting every 3-4 hours during the day and not at all or once a night. At 4 weeks she was dry during the day except when running. Back pain significantly decreased within six weeks. She was on an independent exercise program for the last six weeks. At discharge, she was continent during all activities. She was working full-time and exercising daily without problems.

Erin, 32 years old: Stress Incontinence

Erin, 32 years old, was seen for 3 visits in 4 weeks. Her treatment protocol included the Beyond Kegels Exercise Protocol, including the advanced techniques in standing and breathing. She eliminated caffeine and increased her water consumption. Erin was dry during aerobics within three weeks.

Beth, 59 years old: Urge Incontinence

Beth, 59 years old, was seen for 4 visits. She was totally continent by 3 weeks. Her treatment protocol included adequate fluid intake, no caffeine, daily aerobic exercise for 30 minutes, and the Beyond Kegel Exercise Protocol with adjunctive techniques of physiological quieting and diaphragmatic breathing.

Matilda, 82 years old: Stress Incontinence

Matilda, 82 years old, was seen for 3 visits over a 6-week period. Her treatment protocol included the Beyond Kegel Exercise Protocol, adequate fluid intake, and eliminating caffeine. She changed from tea to hot lemon water. At discharge she was dry at night and usually dry during the day. She wore a mini-pad during the day because she "felt safer that way." She felt confident wearing dresses and going to church or out to lunch with her family.

Robert, 75 years old: Radical Prostatectomy

Robert, 75 years old, was seen for 12 visits over a 9 month period of time. Initially his treatment protocol included adjunctive techniques of physiological quieting and diaphragmatic breathing to quiet the pelvic muscles.

They were in constant contraction in an attempt to stop the leaking. Lifestyle changes included adequate fluid intake and eliminating caffeine. He began taking walks again for 15 minute periods. He rested midday for 45-60 minutes.

Within 3 weeks, Robert was beginning the Beyond Kegels Exercise Protocol. His progress was slow but steady for the next 6 weeks. He could begin to feel the leaks, and his urine stream flow was stronger.

After 8 weeks, Robert was seen every 6-8 weeks for follow up and reinforcement to continue the exercise routine. He continued to have gradually less leaking. After 9 months he was totally dry and had resumed all activities. His only comment was that he had to get his rest or he noticed his urine control was not as good.

Barron, 86 years old: Urge Incontinence

Barron, 86 years old, was seen for 4 visits. He followed the Beyond Kegels Exercise Protocol, increased his fluid intake to 6-8 glasses a day, and practiced spacing his toileting every 2-3 hours. He continued being physically active. Leaking decreased significantly and the explosions were eliminated. He occasionally leaked small amounts with heavy lifting or getting up after sitting in a meeting for several hours.

There are common threads in the programs of all the individuals who shared their stories even though each problem was unique.

All individuals understood the basic concepts of anatomy and function of the urinary system and its interelationship with the bowel and reproductive systems. They understood the neurological connection between the brain, spinal cord and urinary system. They understood the possibilities for voluntary control of the urinary system.

All individuals used self care strategies during daily activities. They became more attentive to what their physical bodies needed. Sometimes it was less caffeine and more clear liquid. Other times it was rest in the middle of the day.

All individuals were reliable carrying out an exercise program on a daily basis. The exercise program re-educated the pelvic muscles to efficiently rest or relax as well as contract appropriately during daily activities. The exercise program strengthened the pelvic muscles so they could support the bladder and bowel in optimum positions for continence.

Most individuals utilized physiological quieting to normalize the tone and function of the bladder (detrusor muscle), and to improve the resting level of pelvic muscles which is as important at the ability to contract or tighten them.

These therapeutic approaches are as good for individuals before they experience a problem as a preventive protocol as for the indivuals with incontinence problems. Many clients say, "I told my friend to start doing the Fabulous Four Exercises now and change her diet now so she won't ever have the problem I have. It's just good sense for long life!"

May you have a long, happy, and active life.

GLOSSARY

Anal Sphincter Two rings of muscles surrounding the rectum and anus which help to control passage of bowel movements.

Anus Muscular opening at the end of the rectum is the outlet for solid waste.

Behavior Therapy Treatment involving conditioning.

Benign Prostatic Hyperplasia (BPH) Condition characterized by growth of a benign tumor inside the prostate, often resulting in voiding difficulties. Also known as benign prostate hypertrophy.

Benign Tumor Noncancerous tissue growth that cannot spread to other areas of the body.

Biopsy Diagnostic procedure of surgically removing a tissue sample from the body and analyzing it microscopically for abnormal tissue growth.

Bladder Muscular organ located inside the pelvis for temporary storage of urine.

Blood Count Test used to determine the number and ratio of red and white blood cells and platelets in an individual's blood. Abnormal numbers can indicate infection, anemia, or cancer.

Blood Tests Samples of individual's blood that can include a blood count, sedimentation rate, glucose level, cholesterol and triglyceride levels, and special tests for prostate cancer (PSA and PAP tests).

Bulbocavernous Muscle One of three muscles of the urogenital diaphragm.

Cancer Disease characterized by uncontrolled cell growth and spread of cells to other parts of the body. Cell growth can crowd out or interfere with normal cell function causing organ dysfunction and death of healthy cells.

Castration Removal of testes or elimination of testicular function with antiandrogen drugs.

Catheter Flexible tube inserted into a body part such as the urethra (in male or female) to empty the bladder of urine.

Cervix Lower portion of the uterus that connects with the vagina.

Chemotherapy Cancer treatment using potent drugs that attack and destroy tissue cells and interfere with the cells multiplying. These drugs are either injected or taken orally.

Clitoris Organ of female orgasm.

Collagen Chemical substance injected into the internal urinary sphincter region to treat incontinence.

Colon Lower portion of large intestine leading to the rectum.

Computerized Tomography (CT scan) A computer-enhanced X-ray technique used to examine soft body tissue.

Congestion Buildup of fluid in an area of the body that often causes pain, i.e., prostate congestion.

Constipation Hard, dry, and firm bowel movements that are difficult to pass and less frequent than normal.

Contraindication Side effects of a medical treatment which would indicate the treatment is more harmful than the intended benefits.

Cryosurgery Surgery that utilizes extreme cold to destroy undesired tissue.

Cystocele Bulging of the bladder into the anterior vaginal wall.

Cystogram Tube with light and a viewing lens at the end, which is inserted into the urethra to examine the urethra, bladder, and prostate gland.

Cystoscopy Diagnostic procedure for urological examination allowing viewing inside the urethra and bladder.

Diagnosis Determination through observation or scientific tests of the existence of symptoms of medical disorders.

Diuretic Any drug, food, or beverage that promotes increased urine excretion.

Encopresis Uncontrolled passage of bowel movement or smears of fecal material into underwear or inappropriate places by an individual over the age of four.

Enterocele A bulging of the pouch of Douglas into the posterior vaginal wall.

Enuresis Involuntary loss of urine, during sleep termed " nocturnal."

Episiotomy Surgical incision into the perineum between the vagina and anus to ease childbirth through the vagina.

Estrogen Hormone contributing to female sex characteristics, produced in female ovaries and male testicles, in adrenal glands, and fat.

Functional Incontinence Physical disability or mental confusion leading to inability to void in an appropriate place.

Hormone Chemical substances made in endocrine glands and essential for human biological processes.

Hormonal Therapy Treatment based on administering hormone or chemical substances that block the action of other hormones. Hormonal therapy blocks action of male hormones that promote tumor growth.

Hysterectomy Surgical removal of the uterus.

Iliococcygeal Muscle One of the muscles forming the pelvic diaphragm/levator ani muscle group.

Impotence Inability of a man to achieve or maintain an erection of sufficient duration.

Incontinence Loss of urinary control.

Intravenous Pyelogram (IVP) Diagnostic procedure to examine the urinary system with X-ray after injecting image-enhancing substances into the bloodstream.

Introitus The external vaginal opening.

Ischiocavernous Muscle One of three muscles forming the urogenital diaphragm.

Ischiococcygeal Muscle Also known as the puborectalis muscle, one of the three muscles forming the pelvic diaphragm/levator ani muscle group.

Kegel Exercises Pelvic muscle exercise to decrease or eliminate incontinence.

Kidneys Two glandular organs that separate waste products from the blood.

Magnetic Resonance Imaging (MRI) Diagnostic technique using an electromagnetic field and computer analysis, which effectively evaluates soft body tissue, such as the prostate and bladder.

Menopause Cessation of menstruation, usually occurs in the late 40's or early 50's.

Orchiectomy Surgical removal of testicles.

Overflow Incontinence Temporary inability to void, followed by uncontrollable urine flow, associated with overdistension of the bladder.

Pelvic Diaphragm The levator ani muscle group.

Pelvic Muscles General term referring to the muscles of the pelvic diaphragm and urogenital diaphragm as one unit, sometimes referred to as the pelvic floor muscles.

Penis The male organ used for urination.

Perineum/Perineal Muscles Area of muscle and tissue between the vagina or scrotum and anus.

Prostate Firm, muscular gland that surrounds the urethra in males.

Prostatectomy Surgical removal of all or part of the prostate gland.

Prostatitis Infection of the prostate; can be acute or chronic.

Pubic Bone Lower front part of the pelvis.

Pubic Symphysis Where the two pubic bones meet.

Pubococcygeal Muscle One of three muscles forming the pelvic diaphragm/levator ani muscle group.

Pudendal Nerve Innervates the external urethral and anal sphincters and the pelvic and urogenital diaphragm muscles; it is part of the voluntary nervous system.

Radiation Therapy X-ray or other high-energy radiation treatment to destroy malignant, cancerous tissue.

Radical Prostatectomy Complete removal of the prostate gland, often used to treat prostate cancer.

Rectocele A bulging of the rectum into the posterior vaginal wall.

Rectum Final several inches of the intestines below the colon and above the anus.

Reflex Incontinence Loss of urine due to hyperactivity of the bladder muscle and/or involuntary urethral relaxation in the absence of the sensation associated with the desire to urinate. This occurs in neurogenic disorders.

Sphincter Circular muscle that tightens and relaxes to control the flow of urine from the urethra. There are internal and external urethral and anal sphincters.

Stress Incontinence Loss of small amounts of urine with increased intra-abdominal pressure during coughing, sneezing, laughing, jumping, running.

Testicles Two glands that produce sperm and sex hormones including testosterone in males (testes).

Testosterone Male sex hormone that is responsible for male sexual characteristics.

Trigone Base of bladder, near bladder neck that is most sensitive area of bladder.

Tumor Body mass caused by abnormal cell growth.

Ultrasound High-frequency sound waves used for medical diagnosis and treatment. An ultrasound scan (sonogram) is sound waves reflected off internal organs to produce computer-enhanced pictures of the bladder, prostate, and urethra.

Urethra Tube connecting the bladder to the outside through which urine is released.

Urethrocele Bulging of the urethra into the vaginal wall.

Urge Incontinence Sudden leaking of relatively large amounts of urine when the bladder muscle contracts, overcoming the contractions of the pelvic and urogenital diaphragm and sphincter muscles.

Urinalysis Tests on urine to diagnose diseases and infections.

Urinary Retention Quantities of urine backing up in the bladder which can cause bladder and kidney damage.

Urinary Tract Infection (UTI) Inflammation or infection in the bladder.

Urogenital Diaphragm Muscles that form the platform for the clitoris; the vagina and urethra pass through it.

Urologist Physician specializing in disorders of the urinary system.

Urology Specialty area of medicine dealing with the disorder of the urinary system.

Uterine Prolapse Descent of the uterus into the vaginal canal.

Uterus Muscular hollow organ that houses the fetus during pregnancy.

Vagina Elastic canal extending from the uterine cervix to the outside. Vaginal walls usually touch but can greatly expand, such as during childbirth.

X-rays Subatomic high energy particle of short wave length that penetrate body tissues to produce photographic images for diagnostic purposes.

WHAT ORGANIZATIONS CAN HELP?

Help for Incontinent People (H.I.P.)
P.O. Box 544
Union, SC 29379
1-800-BLADDER

The Simon Foundation for Continence
P.O. Box 815
Wilmette, IL 60091
1-800-23-SIMON

American Urogynecology Society
401 N. Michigan Ave
Chicago, IL 60611
1-312-644-6610

Section on Women's Health
American Physical Therapy Association
P.O. Box 327
Alexandria, VA 22314
1-703-706-3237

VIDEOTAPES/AUDIOTAPES/BOOKS

Videotape
Endopelvic Exercises:
The Eight Step Guide to Eliminate Incontinence
Phoenix Publishing
P.O. Box 8231
Missoula, Montana 59807

Audiotape
Physiological Quieting
Phoenix Publishing
P.O. Box 8231
Missoula, Montana 59807

Book
Fibromyalgia: A Handbook for Self Care
and Treatment
Phoenix Publishing
P.O. Box 8231
Missoula, Montana 59807

ORDER FORM

I would like to order additional copies of
*Beyond Kegels, Fabulous four exercises and more...
to prevent and treat incontinence.*

1-9 copies $14.95 ea. 10 or more copies $10.95

No. of copies _____ x $14.95 = $ _____

No. of copies _____ x $10.95 = $ _____

Shipping & Handling (1st copy)   = $ 3.50

Each additional copy $.50   = $ _____

Total Cost of Order $ _____

Please send check or money order to
Phoenix Publishing Co.
P.O. Box 8231
Missoula, Montana 59807

Name _____

Address _____

City_____ State _____ Zip _____

Telephone (   ) _____